THE CROWD
FROM
ROARING COVE

by
Bruce Stagg

THE CROWD FROM FROM ROARING COVE

by
Bruce Stagg

Creative Publishers
St. John's, Newfoundland
1997

Cover Art and Design: Bruce Stagg

Second printing: June, 1998

∝ Printed on acid-free paper

Published by
CREATIVE BOOK PUBLISHING
a division of 10366 Newfoundland Limited
a Robinson-Blackmore Printing & Publishing associated company
P.O. Box 8660, St. John's, Newfoundland A1B 3T7

Printed in Canada by:
ROBINSON-BLACKMORE PRINTING & PUBLISHING

Canadian Cataloguing in Publication Data

Stagg, Bruce, 1952-

    The crowd from Roaring Cove

    ISBN 1-895387-80-9

I. Title

PS8587.T26C76 1997   C813'.54   C97-950086-9
PR9199.3.S687C76 1997

Contents

Roaring Cove: An Introduction _ _ _ _ _ _ _ _ _ _ _ _ _ _ _ i

The 1960s _ 1

My Political Rendezvous _ _ _ _ _ _ _ _ _ _ _ _ _ _ _ _ _ 3

Liege Sampson Comes Home _ _ _ _ _ _ _ _ _ _ _ _ _ _ 6

The Devilskin _ 9

A Close Encounter With the Fairies _ _ _ _ _ _ _ _ _ _ 12

Alfie Lambert's Accident _ _ _ _ _ _ _ _ _ _ _ _ _ _ _ 19

Alfie Lambert Improves Health Care _ _ _ _ _ _ _ _ _ 23

Jonas Pickett Goes Mummering _ _ _ _ _ _ _ _ _ _ _ _ 25

Uncle Mark White Goes Cod Jigging _ _ _ _ _ _ _ _ _ 29

Uncle Mark White's Rat _ _ _ _ _ _ _ _ _ _ _ _ _ _ _ _ 33

Jonas Pickett's Tooth _ _ _ _ _ _ _ _ _ _ _ _ _ _ _ _ _ 44

Roaring Cove's Unusual Fire _ _ _ _ _ _ _ _ _ _ _ _ _ 47

My Trip to the Doctor _ _ _ _ _ _ _ _ _ _ _ _ _ _ _ _ _ 51

Our Trip Upalong _ _ _ _ _ _ _ _ _ _ _ _ _ _ _ _ _ _ _ 54

The Hypochondriac _ _ _ _ _ _ _ _ _ _ _ _ _ _ _ _ _ _ 62

The Pop-Up Toaster _ _ _ _ _ _ _ _ _ _ _ _ _ _ _ _ _ _ 66

A Tribute to Silas Murphy _ _ _ _ _ _ _ _ _ _ _ _ _ _ _ 69

Silas Murphy Gets Arrested _ _ _ _ _ _ _ _ _ _ _ _ _ _ 79

The Squatting Stick _ _ _ _ _ _ _ _ _ _ _ _ _ _ _ _ _ _ 82

Jonas Pickett Takes His Turn as Church Sexton _ _ _ _ _ _ _ 85

Crime in Roaring Cove _ _ _ _ _ _ _ _ _ _ _ _ _ _ _ _ 88

Uncle Mark White Goes Moose Hunting _ _ _ _ _ _ _ _ 92

The Blowing Hole _ _ _ _ _ _ _ _ _ _ _ _ _ _ _ _ _ _ _ 95

"Aunt Daisy's Spuds" _ _ _ _ _ _ _ _ _ _ _ _ _ _ _ _ _ 109

Roaring Cove: An Introduction

Surrounded by the North Atlantic brine, every Newfoundland shoreline is trimmed with a horizon, giving it the prestigious honour of being isolated. With its distinct borders of high granite cliffs shrouded in silvery fog, this island exists alone like a triangle pushed off the page of a geometry book. Within these borders, thousands of tiny outport villages lie nestled in the safety of Newfoundland's many bays, coves and inlets.

Typical of its siblings, Roaring Cove clings like a puffin's nest to the cliffs that surround Roaring Cove Harbour. Only to the entrance of the harbour did Mother Nature show any compassion to this coastline. A split in the cliff, barely a gunshot across, gives entrance to a fiord or an arm that penetrates the earth for about a mile, giving safe haven to the little fishing boats and the brightly-coloured homes of Roaring Cove.

Just inside the harbour entrance, a wide beach of eroded rocks that resemble bowling balls escort the waves ashore and disperse them into a foamy surf before they are sucked back out to sea by the undertow. With each action of each wave, the large stones tumble over each other, creating a roaring sound that echoes the mood of the sea off the cliffs behind the beach. It is this sound from which Roaring Cove acquired its name.

Just beyond the beach, a point of land, known as Manuel's Point, juts into the fiord like a finger. This is where the first settlers of Roaring Cove built their homes in order to be close to the fishing grounds. Manuel's Point quickly became overcrowded, and other settlers were forced to build their homes wherever the land allowed access to the sea. Consequently, houses were built all the way along the south side of the harbour, from Manuel's Point to where Bakeapple Marsh River runs into the bottom of the fiord. The north side of the harbour was never built up, and never will be, because the cliffs drop straight into the water.

In the early 1960s, a gravel road was built through Bakeapple Marsh Valley, and Roaring Cove was connected to other outports by a cloud of dust. The road was chiselled into the cliff, and it meandered its way along the south side hills to the very last house in the harbour. The cliffs were too steep, though, for the road to reach Manuel's Point, so houses that had stood for generations were launched on forty-five-gallon oil drums and floated in the arm. The only house left was Tacker Manuel's old house on the tip of the point. Tacker figured that the house could not survive the transplant, so he sold it to Jonas Pickett. You see, Jonas, who is well known in Roaring Cove as bit of a sleeveen,* was too cantankerous to mix with people on a daily basis, so he chose to remain on Manuel's Point by himself. He lives there to this day, without electricity or any other modern conveniences.

This was the first house I saw as I entered Roaring Cove Harbour on board the coastal steamer several years ago. I kept looking for the rest of the community, thinking, "How abandoned the house looks, standing alone and surrounded only by the grassy impressions of a few old root cellars that rise like tombs out of the vacant fields!"

When we rounded the point, though, there it was: a splatter of bright colours against a dark grey backdrop, a

---

* A sly, deceitful person

picture elegant enough to adorn any artist's canvas. This was Roaring Cove, the place that was about to become my home. I had come to Roaring Cove on a one-year teaching assignment. Little did I know that the warmth and hospitality, bored into these cliffs, would keep me there.

As the steamer slowly made its way deeper into the harbour, the details of the community became more evident. Bright red, green, orange, yellow and turquoise houses looked like they were merely stuck to the cliff. From each, a footpath wound its way down the cliff to slate-grey fishing stages and stores. A man sculling a rodney up along the shore waved a greeting to the steamer. The vessel responded with two quick blasts of its whistle. I learned later that it was Toby Avery, making a trip out to his lobster vat.

I scanned the community for the schoolhouse, locating it just below the little church that stood high on the cliffs and overlooked the community and the sea. As we steamed past the school, I noticed that it was built on what appeared to be the only flat piece of land in the place—a sort of plateau to the cliff that rose from the water. The little two-room schoolhouse was an old building, but I could tell from the lustre of the snow-white paint and the sharpness of the bright red trim that it had been freshly painted. It had two large windows facing the water. Each consisted of a grid of several smaller square windows like the blocks of a chocolate bar. I noticed that the windows were not aligned with each other. Instead, they drooped on the inward corners, making the schoolhouse appear as if it were frowning. This was the building in which I would begin my career, and the one in which I would spend many happy, memorable years.

Looking to the bottom of the fiord, I could see the bridge that crosses Bakeapple Marsh River, as well as where the river empties into the harbour. Beyond the river was the government wharf. Painted white with the railings, side ladders and grumps* trimmed in bright red, it somewhat resembled a peppermint knob sticking into the harbour. A small number of onlookers had gathered on the wharf to meet the boat and to see what strange cargo she might be carrying. As we docked, I surveyed the inquisitive crowd. They were all strange faces to me then, but soon they would become as close as family.

A man in a legionnaire's blazer and tam was standing at the head of the wharf. He shouted some docking instruction to the steamer's captain and quickly boarded the ship as soon as the gangplank was lowered, going directly to the bridge. It was Uncle Mark White. I was not to see him again until one day in the fall when he showed up on my front steps and invited me to his house for a salmon dinner. He and his wife, Aunt Mae, were to become like parents to me.

A woman wearing a full-length apron and a bandanna tied tightly around her head was chastising some youngsters for playing too closely to the head of the wharf. I soon learned that she was Roaring Cove's hypochondriac, Aunt Daisy Snelgrove. Later, after I purchased my car, I was to become Aunt Daisy's private taxi back and forth to the hospital in Middleville.

The children, who were playing on the head of the wharf, were throwing sticks into the water, and a golden Labrador retriever, Old Jack, was jumping into the water and proudly fetching sticks for them. The ringleader of the crowd was a

---

* A wooden post on a wharf to which boats are tied

little blond, curly-haired boy. All too soon I would get to know him as Alfie Lambert, Roaring Cove's devilskin.[*]

Across the road from the wharf was the general store. A man in a suit, white shirt, and necktie left the store, carrying a parcel wrapped in brown paper. He walked briskly onto the wharf and brought the parcel straight on board the steamer. It was Sam Whiffen, the owner of the general store and the fish merchant here in Roaring Cove.

When I stepped on the wharf, a black car pulled up and a clergyman stepped out. I knew he had to be the Reverend King, because he had informed me by telegram that he would meet me at the steamer and take me to the teacher's residence. He extended his hand to me, helped store my luggage in his car trunk, and sped me away to my new home.

It is about this place and these people I tell my stories.

---

[*] A mischievous person, practical joker

The 1960s

Yes, sir, Uncle Mark White thinks that all this gloom and doom that everyone is feeling about the cod moratorium is bunkum,* and I'm half inclined to agree with him. Sure, it was the same thing in the 1960s—everyone was convinced that the fish had disappeared and would never return. Many a Newfoundlander was forced to lay off fishing and move away for awhile, as they are being forced to move away today.

"Burn your boats!" was the big cry of the 1960s. Aunt Daisy Snelgrove, deaf on her left side since birth, heard "Burn your goats!" Unwilling to doubt the creator of this infamous quote, the late Joseph R. Smallwood, a man whom she worshipped, she doused Albert, her old yellow-whiskered billy goat, with kerosene oil and set him afire. Poor old Albert shot over Aunt Daisy's back fence like a lightening bolt and crawled away under Johnny Eddy's back porch. Fanning the flames as he dashed across the garden, he barbecued himself—and burned Johnny's house to the ground.

Others were not so lucky; born with two good ears, they ended up in Toronto. Boys and girls straight out of school, sealers, boat builders, and shopkeepers alike went to work in

---

* Nonsense

the morning by subway and cursed those whose breath smelled of garlic. Summers brought them home religiously, with their 440 convertibles and upalong accents. They taught us that it was fashionable to wear baseball caps with favourite beer labels on the front, that we lived in houses and not 'ouses, and that it was impolite to pick one's nose in public and unsanitary to pick it in private. When they went back to Toronto, they brought salt fish, bakeapples,* salt beef, hard tack**—and relatives. Roaring Cove was left to the old folks and those who didn't have the guts—or the heart—to move.

Every Sunday from the pulpit, the Rev. King prayed for family members living away, and Uncle Mark prophesied better times ahead. Uncle Mark was right—he was always right—and he would be right again.

---

* A cloudberry that grows on the bogs. It ripens in early to mid August and is usually used to make jam.
** A hard sea biscuit that is kiln dried and baked into solid cakes— popular as a snack

My Political Rendezvous

A few years back, the Government decided that it was too expensive to maintain the school here in Roaring Cove and that it would be in the best interest of education to bus the youngsters all the way to Middleville. As it was an election year, Thumb-On-Wrench Swyers, chairman of the local school committee, figured that the best way for us to save our school was to elect a government member from right here in the place. Thumb-On-Wrench, so-called because he had been born with a deformed hand and because he owned the only garage in the place, convinced me that I stood the best chance of getting elected. And thus began my political rendezvous.

No, I did not get elected, but I sure did learn a lot about our Newfoundland people. I equate my experience to a university degree in philosophy or sociology.

I'll never forget the day I was campaigning up in Kellop Harbour. I approached an old gentleman who was sitting on the cuddy* of his punt.** He was small and thin, with a long narrow nose, hollow cheeks and beady eyes. He wore a tattered bibbed cap that was supported by large flaring ears.

As I approached him, he picked up the piggin*** and

---

* A compartment built in the front of a boat.
** A small open fishing boat.
***A container used to bail water from a boat

began bailing water, pretending not to notice me. I extended my hand into the boat and made a bid for the vote I had come to secure. He reluctantly offered me his hand. It was dirt-grained, calloused and deeply browned by the sun. I thought it would nip and bite into my flesh like a rusty claw of a wrench. Instead, it was limp and rubbery, and it gave a sensation similar to when one picks up a dead codfish that has been baking in the sun.

Feeling the superiority of my grip, I announced Kellop Harbour's share from my little bag of election goodies. There was a half mile of pavement, a ten-foot extension to the wharf, a new porch for the Fisherman's Hall, a fence for the playground, and a student clean-up project.

The gentleman was unimpressed. He came to his feet, settled back on his heels, and gave his cap a vicious twist, like he was locking it into place. He grabbed the boat hook from the rising,* swung it high above his shoulder, and sunk it into the wharf but inches from my foot. Using it as a handle, he was standing in front of me in the time it takes to swallow an Adam's apple rising in one's throat. He jerked his chin parallel to his chest, threw his nose into the air, and fired a spit into the water. Tapping his index finger on his chest like a needle bobbing in a sewing machine, he rapped out every syllable of his attack.

"What gives you the right to go struttin' over my stage with your high-falutin' ideas and your vote-buyin' hand-outs?" he yelled. "Santa Claus! You come down here like Santa Claus with a wish list, and you end up fillin' the stockings with junk. We got no time for your promises here

---

* A board around the inside of a boat which determines the boats shape.

in Kellop Harbour, me son, so the best thing for you to do is to take yer arse in ya hand and retrace yer steps. I'd just as soon take the gun and shoot the bloody lot of ye. Certainly, it would be a sin to waste good number four shot on ye! I'd say the best thing would be to load her up with knobs of shit and fire that at ye!"

I was somewhat stunned and taken aback and, for something more appropriate to say, I said, "Well, Sir, I'll put you down as 'doubtful'."

As I turned to leave, I caught the hint of a gleam in the gentleman's eye. "God bless you, me son," he said. "God bless you."

Liege Sampson Comes Home

Since this cod moratorium has been on, people have been packing up and heading out. Some say that places like Roaring Cove will be no more. Uncle Mark White, an authority on everything that goes on in Roaring Cove, says it is all bunkum. It has never been any different in Roaring Cove—men have always had to move away, and the times have always been hard. It all started 'way back in the 1920s when many a good Newfoundlander had to pack in the punt and head out for the prosperous United States of America. According to Uncle Mark, it wasn't their moving away that caused the problem, it was their coming home.

Liege Sampson was the first man to return from the States. He stepped off the steamer with a pair of well-worn boxing gloves slung over his shoulder, the first ones ever seen in Roaring Cove. Liege boasted that he had sparred with the likes of Jack Dempsey, and claimed that he too could have been a boxing champion if the good Lord had seen fit to give him a bigger frame.

Oh, Liege had acquired some boxing skills, all right. The only problem was that every time he got a few drinks in—which was quite often—he went around picking a fight with whomever happened to be close. For years, every soup supper, card game or time of any sort ended up in a racket, with Liege always being the instigator.

Well, one night, at the supper after the Fisherman's parade, Liege picked a fight with Uncle Mark. The latter was a small person who had an opinion on everything. He was not known to cause trouble, but he never walked away from it either. When Liege bullied and challenged him, Uncle Mark stood his ground. Liege threw the first smack, which caught Uncle Mark on the bridge of his nose, sending a splatter of blood over the white tablecloth. Liege's next blow sent Uncle Mark sprawling to the floor among the chairs. Before the older man could get up, Liege was on him, pounding him mercilessly, one smack after the other. The dull thud of flesh striking flesh sent children running in all directions. It took six or seven of the most able men and women to drag Liege off and hold him while Uncle Mark made his escape by crawling under the tables.

When they were reasonably sure that Uncle Mark had time enough to make his getaway, they released Liege. As they did, Uncle Mark surfaced on the other side of the hall, calling for a bayonet.

"I didn't fight overseas to be bullied by the likes of you, Liege Sampson," Uncle Mark said, "and if I had a bayonet, I'd run yer through!"

Then Uncle Mark reached into his pocket and made a fist around his unopened pocketknife. His temper now at a boiling point, he danced across the floor, swinging his arms wildly. Liege cocked his fist in an impressive-looking boxing pose and made a couple of quick jabs at his attacker, but

Uncle Mark was flicking around the floor like a tomcod* that had landed on a dry stagehead and Liege completely missed his mark.

Uncle Mark connected with one lucky blow, striking Liege just above his left temple with the butt of his unopened pocketknife. Liege came to four days later. He never fought again, and order was once again restored to Roaring Cove. It wasn't because Liege had learned a lesson, though, but because every time he drank after that he got giddy and blacked out.

---

* A young codfish.

The Devilskin

No one knew better than I just what a devilskin Alfie Lambert was. There were times when he was in school when he almost gave me a nervous breakdown. He was forever up to some kind of mischief. I remember one time in particular. I was doing a Remembrance Day concert with my class. Alfie wanted nothing to do with it, but I expected all students to participate. So I insisted he take a part, the same as everyone else.

I gave him the smallest part in the skit—the role of the padre. His one and only line was to ask the audience for a moment of silence to remember the dead. Although it was unnecessary for the padre to dress in costume, I insisted that he wear the Reverend King's big, high, purple hat—the one the minister always wore at special Easter ceremonies. Consequently, Alfie looked silly and out of place—and he knew it. I knew it too, but I thought it appropriate—sweet revenge for all the times Alfie had tormented me.

To tell the truth, I never really expected Alfie to show up for the concert, and I was somewhat surprised when he did, especially when he donned the funny-looking hat without protest and took to the stage. What I didn't know, of course, was that Alfie was up to his mischief again; he had a plan to sabotage the minute of silence. You see, Alfie had brought an alarm clock from home, and before he went on stage, he set the alarm and put the clock up in his hat.

When Alfie's turn came, he stepped forward and, in his best and most audible voice and in a tone of deep reverence, he said his piece, "And now, ladies and gentlemen, I ask you all to join with me in a minute of silence for those who bravely laid down their lives for the freedom of all mankind." Alfie then folded his arms across his chest and closed his eyes in sombre silence. The audience followed his lead and did the same. I was extremely pleased with Alfie's seriousness, a side of him I hadn't seen before.

About twenty seconds after, the silence was ominously shattered by the clanging ring of an alarm clock! Everyone was startled and began looking for the source of the sound. All eyes fell on Alfie, and a devious grin formed on his face. The audience began to giggle; the most serious moment of the skit was ruined. The clock continued to sound and the smile on Alfie's face broadened—sweet revenge for him.

A few seconds later, though, I noticed the grin leave his face. His mouth gaped open, his chin jutted forward, and the sinews in his neck tightened and became visible. The audience now broke into uproarious laughter.

"Alfie's making faces at the audience," I thought. He was carrying it too far now, so I reached for the drawstring to close the curtain. As I did, Alfie let out a loud scream, ripped the hat from his head, and threw it on the floor. The audience laughed hysterically when they saw the clock on Alfie's head, entangled in his mop of curly, blond hair. From where I was standing, I could see his hair being twisted around the keys and pulled into the innermost workings of the clock.

Alfie grabbed the clock with both hands and yelled, "Shut it off!" The look on his face was one of pure agony as he twisted wildly at the clock, unsure of which way to turn it to relieve the pressure. I closed the curtain and went to Alfie's rescue. His face was twisted grotesquely out of shape, and he begged me to stop the clock. I tried to reach the shut-off button on the back, but couldn't because the clock had drawn itself too tightly to Alfie's scalp.

"Get the scissors!" he yelled. "Cut it out quick!"

I ran to hunt down a pair of scissors, but by the time I got back, the clock had run itself down and Alfie's face looked like it had a nylon stocking stretched over it. I liberally began to snip away at his blond curls. As I did, his hair fell about his face and into his eyes. "Close your eyes," I commanded.

"I can't," Alfie groaned. "I don't have enough slack skin!"

A Close Encounter With the Fairies

I came out of the post office this morning and bumped into Uncle Mark White. It was by far the hottest day we had had in Roaring Cove in several years, and Uncle Mark was leaning over the post office bridge, in the shade of the old dogberry tree.

"Hot enough for you, Uncle Mark?" I asked.

"Not healthy, me son, not healthy," he replied.

Uncle Mark's braces were hanging down around his hips, and his shirt and underwear top were unbuttoned to his navel. The tan line around his neck made his chest and belly show up white like the underside of a flatfish.

"Wouldn't be goin' down the road, would you?" he asked. "It's too hot fer an old feller like me to be walkin'."

Of course, I was only too happy to oblige Uncle Mark with a ride, and besides, I sort of figured I'd get a story out of it. I wasn't disappointed. Somewhere in the course of the conversation, the topic changed from hot weather to cold. It was on the cold weather that he launched his story. I just kept quiet and took it all in.

"The coldest time I ever felt in me life was the winter of 1948," he began. "Besides the below-normal temperatures, the doctor informed me that me blood was low—not enough of the right kind of grub, I s'pose. Well, Sir, in spite of the cold, most of the Roarin' Cove men flocked to the lumberwoods. We all wanted a share of the paltry few dollars that two months of hard cuttin' and pilin' would bring—yes, everyone, including Jonas Pickett.

"Next to the cold temperatures and the camp grub, it was Jonas I remember most about that winter. Jonas, you see, was a big man—and lazy. Everyone in Roarin' Cove knew that old Jonas was the laziest that God ever put breath into. And, he was the clumsiest thing you ever saw trying to get on the right end of a stick; the boys 'llowed that he cut about half a cord a day. It was only natural, I s'pose, that he would end up on the butt end of all our funnin' that winter. Jobie Rodgers started in on him the minute he boarded the train.

"'So,'" said Jobie, "'you're gonna give the lumberwoods a try, is ya, Jonas? S'pose you knows the grub is awful bad. Great time to lose a bit of weight, Jonas, boy. You'll be eatin' baked beans three times a day, seven days a week.'

"Jonas just slired* up at Jobie from underneath the bib of his cap. I kept my mouth shut because I knew that old Jonas Pickett could be as saucy as a hungry crackie** if he wanted to be.

"'S'pose you heard about the crowd that went in last winter, did you, Jonas?' Jobie asked, not about to back off by a mere slire. 'Yep, Jonas, boy, twenty-two of them went up in the box of a woods truck, and they all came down in the cab.' Then Jobie let out three or four big laughs to let the rest of the boys know that he had gotten one on old Jonas.

---

* A dirty look.
** A mongrel dog.

"Well, that started it. It went on from there for the rest of the winter. Sometimes I even felt sorry for Jonas, but the things he did to avoid work! He hurt his back, he had several bouts with the 'flu and two cases of pneumonia, and once he cut his foot with the axe—he claimed the axe glanced off a frozen log. He had us all feeling sorry for him with his bad foot—as nasty a cut as you'd ever want to see, right across the instep, just above the toes. With nothing but a bit of iodine and mercurochrome to put in it, we were all afraid that gangrene would set in. We even laid off him for awhile.

"Anyway, Jonas demanded to see the supervisor; he wanted to be sent home on compensation. And what else could the super do? The foot was festered up and ugly looking. Well, to make a long story short, all arrangements were made, and Jonas was to be sent home on full compensation.

"Albert Hicks spotted it. I would never have noticed it in a hundred years and, if I had, I think I would have kept it to myself. Jonas was about to leave and was trying to get his bad foot down in his boot. 'Is that the boots you had on when you cut your foot, Jonas?' Albert asked.

"'The only pair I got,' Jonas replied.

"'Well, dat must have been some sharp axe!' Albert added. 'Went right through yer boot, cut yer foot, but never left a mark on the boot.'

"The bunkhouse went up in laughter; everyone was in stitches, except for Jonas—and the super who happened to walk in at the right moment. Now, I have seen many a man get a good tongue bangin', but this was the head. Poor old Jonas never opened his mouth; he just crawled away in the corner of his bunk, like a puppy after dirtin' on the floor. Needles to say, Jonas spent the rest of the year with us, and we heard nothin' else about his bad foot or any other ailment, for that matter. Nevertheless, the jokes and tormentin' continued to be aimed at Jonas.

"I remember one night in particular. It was a sin what Jobie Rodgers did, but I still laughs when I thinks about it. It was a vicious cold night in February, and we were sittin' around the bunkhouse, spinnin' a few ghost yarns, the usual Saturday night entertainment.

"Gideon Forward was the ringleader. He claimed that he had some kind of link to the supernatural because he was lost in the woods when he was a youngster. Missing for five days, he was. Claimed that the fairies found him wanderin' around a big bog and took him to a place in the deep woods and cared for him until the search party found him.

"This made Gideon Forward an authority on anything that mysteriously went missing. And around the room it went, stories about mysterious disappearances—everything from Aunt Daisy Snelgrove's chamber pot to Saul Blackmore's wife. Each man had a story that would send a tingle down your spine—everyone, except Jonas Pickett. He just sat there and took it all in. Jobie 'llowed that Jonas was too afraid to draw his breath.

"About half past ten, it was, and we was gettin' a scattered 'Listen! What's that noise?' and 'Where's me pipe to?' when Jonas took with a hard stomach cramp—the baked beans, most likely.

"'Anyone want to make a trip down to the outhouses?' he asked. There was dead silence as glances were exchanged around the room. You see, we all knew what old Jonas was up to. The outhouses were down in the woods, across the clearin' from the bunkhouse, and Jonas was afraid to go down there by himself.

"'No, way, Jonas,' answered Gideon. 'You wouldn't catch me down there tonight. There's a full moon, you know, and on a full moon the fairies do play.'

"The rest of the men totally ignored Jonas and went on with their storytellin'. But Jonas didn't budge; he stayed on the edge of his bunk, until he was all doubled over with the cramp. Finally, he could stand it no longer. Without saying a word, he grabbed his parka and took off through the door.

"'I'll bet a cord of wood he'll never go down to them toilets tonight,' bellowed a voice from the back of the bunk-house. Now, nobody dared to answer that bet because we all knew what Jonas would do. And sure enough, we watched him to about the middle of the clearin' when off he scooted down behind the bunkhouse.

"Quick as a conner* snatchin' the bait off a hook, Jobie grabbed the square-topped coal shovel and gave it to her out the back door. He cut off Jonas down by the big pile of firewood. Jonas had his parka off and was pullin' down his braces as he was runnin.' It looked like he was tryin' to make it down behind the woodpile, but he couldn't hold out, so down he squatted in the droke** of a small birch. That was just dandy for Jobie. He hopped in the droke, circled down around, and came up behind Jonas. There was a good frost crust on the snow, so Jobie could slide over it without makin' a sound.

"As soon as Jonas got down to business and started to grunt, Jobie slipped the shovel into position. Now, although Jonas didn't know it, his aim was dead on—right in the

---

* An ocean perch found around fishing wharves—catching conners is a favourite sport of Newfoundland children.
** A small spot of woods, usually consisting of one type of tree.

shovel. When Jobie was sure that Jonas had finished, he pulled the shovel back and tucked himself away to await the fun.

"With a sigh of relief, Jonas slued his head and took a look. He couldn't believe what he was seein'—or wasn't seein', I should say. For a moment, he was stunned; he stayed squattin' down, with his chin hangin' over his left shoulder and his eyes searchin' the snow. Suddenly, he spun himself around on the slippery snow, fell to his knees, and gave the place proper inspection. He even ran the palm of his hand over the spot, as if lookin' for cracks in the snow that might have opened up and engulfed it. Then it dawned on him. 'Fairies!' he shouted. With one swift movement, he blessed himself three times with one hand, grabbed his pants at the knees with the other, and took off for the bunkhouse.

"The rest of us nearly split our sides with laughter when Jonas came burstin' into the bunkhouse, with his pants around his knees and swearin' to the good Man above that *it* had disappeared. Gideon Forward listened with a keen ear as Jonas gave the details, confirmin' that Jonas had had himself one close encounter with the fairies.

"Yes, Sir, Jonas might not have cut much wood that winter, but he sure made the fun for the rest of us. I'll always remember it as the year my blood was low and Jonas Pickett went to the lumberwoods."

Twenty minutes later, I'm still parked in front of Uncle Mark's gate, wiping the tears and sweat from my face. Uncle Mark is sitting half in the car and half out; his deodorant has completely broken down, and he's getting ready to launch another story.

"Come in the house and have a cup of tea," he said, "and

I'll tell ye about the time Jonas filled the rum barrel half full of water."

"Not now, Uncle Mark," I said. "Save it for another time—besides, it's too hot for tea."

Alfie Lambert's Accident

Roaring Cove has been buzzing all this week with news of how Old Jack saved Alfie Lambert's life. Nobody knows who owns Old Jack or where he came from. You see, Old Jack is Roaring Cove's dog, a golden Labrador retriever that roams from door to door, collecting table scraps. He usually follows the children around and when they throw sticks into the water, he promptly retrieves the sticks and drops them at their feet.

The story of Alfie's accident goes like this. Last Saturday, Thumb-on-Wrench Swyers was working in his garage when Old Jack showed up with Alfie's cap in his mouth. Old Jack tugged on the leg of Thumb-On-Wrench's coveralls until the latter followed him down across Bakeapple Marsh, in behind Roaring Cove Pond. It was there that Thumb-On-Wrench found Alfie lying unconscious in the bog. Alfie had a serious burn to the back of his head and his right hand was badly mangled. Rumours of foul play ran rampant. There was even talk that Alfie had been abducted by aliens, subjected to some kind of torture, and dropped off on the marsh.

On Wednesday, Alfie regained consciousness and put an end to the rumours—he had been hit by lightening, which had struck him in the back of his head, travelled through his body, and burst out through his hand. The doctors in Middleville said he was lucky to be alive. But Uncle Mark White said, "A likely story."

Now, I knew that Uncle Mark was not about to let something as mysterious as this drop and, sure enough, the day before yesterday, he called me up and told me he had been down on Bakeapple Marsh, looking at the spot where Alfie Lambert had been found.

"What did you find?" I asked.

"Plenty," he replied. "If you're not doing anything tomorrow, I'll take you down there and show ya."

The next morning, the fog was lying heavy in Bakeapple Marsh Valley, so it was almost lunchtime before we got on the way. When Uncle Mark came out of his house, he had Old Jack with him.

"Mind if Old Jack comes along?" Uncle Mark asked.

"Not at all," I replied, pushing open the car door. Old Jack jumped into the back seat, sat up, and looked out the window, like any passenger.

I parked behind Thumb-On-Wrench's garage, and the three of us set out over the barrens, the same way that Old Jack had led Thumb-On-Wrench. When we reached the marsh, Uncle Mark led me to the spot where Alfie had been found, and Old Jack sniffed around the spot, wagging his tail in excitement.

"There's nothing to be seen here," I commented.

"No," said Uncle Mark, "but come over here." And he led me to the edge of the bog, where a well-worn path cut through the woods.

"Alfie was injured down by the river," Uncle Mark said, "and he followed this path with the intention of cutting up across the marsh, but he collapsed here. Now, follow me."

We followed the path through a narrow droke of woods

and, in no time, we broke out on the riverbank by the salmon pool.

"Now, look here," Uncle Mark said, pointing to a spot on the riverbank that was obviously scorched. All around were tiny pieces of white plastic and larger pieces of half melted black electrical tape.

"So this is where the lightning hit," I said. "But what are all these plastic bits?"

Uncle Mark did not answer. He was standing on a rock by the side of the river. "Look here," he said, pointing into the salmon pool.

Immediately, I saw the dark water swirl, and I caught the silver flash of a feeding salmon. As I stared more intently into the pool, in the shadow of the rocky ledge I noticed the gentle swaying of, not one, but many salmon. "Why, the pool's full of salmon!" I observed with excitement.

"Exactly," said Uncle Mark. "Do you know what the old fellers did when they caught salmon in the pool like that?" he asked.

"I can't imagine," I commented.

"They would dynamite the river—that's what."

"How?" I asked.

"Easy," Uncle Mark said. "All that was needed was a small stick of dynamite—about this size." With that, he pulled a small wooden stick from his pocket. "Next," he continued, "the dynamite would have to be waterproofed." And, from another pocket, he pulled out a white plastic shopping bag and a roll of electrical tape. He carefully wrapped the stick up in the plastic bag, coiling endless layers of tape around it. "Now, it's a simple matter of lighting the fuse and tossing the dynamite into the pool," he said.

Uncle Mark lit the imaginary fuse with an imaginary

match and threw the mock dynamite into the pool. It had no sooner left his hand when Old Jack took chase. In no time, he was swimming towards me, with his fetch in his mouth.

"Now," said Uncle Mark, "Old Jack is retrieving a live stick of dynamite to ya. Whatta ya gonna do?"

I felt the urgency of the situation. My first instinct was to run, but I thought about Old Jack being blown to kingdom come. "I don't know," I said.

"What would Alfie have done, if 'twas him?" Uncle Mark asked.

Then it dawned on me and I saw the point of Uncle Mark's little charade. He was reenacting what had happened to Alfie Lambert, so I played along. Alfie, I knew, would have taken any risk to save Old Jack. So, I did what he would have—or had—done. I frantically called Old Jack to me and retrieved the package from his mouth. I drew back my arm, with the intention of slinging the dynamite halfway to Kellop Harbour. As I did, Uncle Mark grabbed my hand and held it.

"S'pose it exploded now!" he stated. "Imagine the mangling to your hand and the burn to the back of your head."

"And the little bits of plastic that would be strewn around," I said, kicking at the scorched spot on the ground.

Uncle Mark and I were silent for the longest time. It was he who spoke first. "Schoolmaster," he said, "I think it best if we keep this between the two of us."

Alfie Lambert Improves Health Care

Alfie Lambert had been in the hospital in Middleville for almost two weeks with a nasty burn to the back of his head and his right hand. He claims he was struck by lightning while crossing Bakeapple Marsh. However, Uncle Mark White and I have another explanation for his injuries, but we see no need to broadcast it all over the place.

As we always do when someone from Roaring Cove is in the hospital, Uncle Mark and I went to Middleville to visit Alfie, who was vigorously complaining about the standard of health care the hospital was providing. He told us that he was on a ward with nine or ten other men, and it was pure madness. "The poor nurses are literally run off their feet," he said. The IV bags were always empty and the bedpans always full. And, in the night, Alfie noticed that there was only one nurse on duty to cover the entire ward. He said that she was like a soldier, sent to fight a war by herself. I daresay that's exactly how she felt. And, I daresay that if she wins her war, some government official will pin a medal on his own chest. On the other hand, should she lose the war, it will be the nurse who will be court-martialled.

Alfie said he felt sorry for the nurse and tried to help her out as much as he could by doing for himself and by helping to lift Mr. Spurrell, the 250-pound patient in the next bed, onto his bedpan.

Alfie wondered what would happen in the case of an emergency. Then, he figured that an emergency was the very thing that was needed to open a few eyes, so he created one. A master of devilment, he created a commotion that caused the hospital administrator to rule that at least two nurses were required on night duty at all times.

What Alfie did was to empty the entire contents of an eight-ounce bottle of ENO effervescing powder into Mr. Spurrell's bedpan. Sometime during the night, Alfie and the nurse lifted Mr. Spurrell onto the bedpan. When he made his water, it began to fizzle and sparkle. It hissed and gurgled, bubbling over the rim of the pan and into the bed. The poor man went hysterical with fright and kept yelling that his bladder had exploded! The nurse had no idea of what was happening and was at a loss about how to handle the situation. She called a code one emergency. By the time the on-call nurses and doctors got to Mr. Spurrell, it was realized that, if it had been a real emergency, the poor man surely would have died.

Jonas Pickett Goes Mummering

Last Saturday was a bitterly cold day, with northwest wind and drifting snow. Around ten o'clock in the morning, I looked out through my kitchen window and noticed Uncle Mark White crippling across the harbour ice, with a little package tucked underneath his arm. He went straight out from the government wharf and landed on Manuel's Point. "Strange," I thought. "There's nothing out on Manuel's Point, only Jonas Pickett. And why in the world would Uncle Mark be visiting Jonas? Jonas made it perfectly clear years ago that he wanted to be left alone."

I hadn't much else to do, so I sat down at the window, with a cup of tea in my hand, and listened to the radio. In about an hour, I saw Uncle Mark working his way back across the harbour ice. He now had to butt the wind and, with the ice as slippery as it was, he was making little headway. So, he took to the land down by the school bus turn-around. Thinking I'd save him a long walk up through the community, I jumped aboard my car and went to pick him up.

Uncle Mark's cheeks were blotchy red from the cold and wind, and a small drip was hanging from the tip of his nose. He settled into the front seat. I didn't have to ask what he was up to; he volunteered the information.

"I just came in from Manuel's Point," he said.

"I know," I responded. "I saw you crossing the ice. I saw when you went ashore, too, so I thought I'd come down and give you a lift."

"Much obliged," he said, wiping the drop from his nose with the back of his cuff. "I went out to see Jonas Pickett. Mae made a pot of fresh beef soup, and I brought him out a drop."

Now, I knew for sure there was something strange going on. "You brought soup out to Jonas Pickett?" I asked with amazement.

"Yes, he has a bad bout of pneumonia, you know," Uncle Mark said in a tone of concern.

"Still," I said, "you're the last person I'd ever expect to be nursing old Jonas." I knew, you see, that there was no love lost between Uncle Mark White and Jonas Pickett. Over the years, they had fallen out a dozen times, and I had often heard Uncle Mark refer to Jonas as "the laziest and most miserable person ever to draw a drop of breath."

"Well, I feel sort of responsible for him being sick," Uncle Mark mumbled.

"What do you mean—you feel responsible for Jonas being sick?" I asked.

"Well," said Uncle Mark, "you remember Old Christmas Night when you telephoned and told me to lock me doors and turn off the lights because Jonas was going around mummering again?"

"Yes," I said. Now, I could clearly recall what Uncle Mark was referring to. You see, every year on the last day of Christmas—Old Christmas Day—Jonas comes in the harbour mummering. It's the only time he ever visits anyone, and everyone knows why he does it. The mummering tradition in Roaring Cove is the same as it is in all Newfoundland communities. People disguise themselves in costume and go from house to house, challenging the owners to identify them. Once identified, the mummer is treated to a Christmas toddy. This was Jonas' way of getting a few free drinks. He wore the same costume each year, so it wasn't hard to recognize him. He always pulled an old, one-piece suit of long-john underwear over his snowsuit, and stuffed it with pillows. Then he pulled a blanket over his head to hide his face. But everyone guessed him immediately and gave him his drink, just to get rid of him.

On the night Uncle Mark was talking about, Jonas had had enough to drink when he got to my house. I identified him immediately and gave him his drink. He poured out almost a full glass of rum and drank it straight down. When he left, he was staggering, and he said that he was heading for Uncle Mark's house, so I called Uncle Mark and warned him.

"Well, I let him in," said Uncle Mark. "When you called and said he was on 'is way, I figured I'd fix him once and fer all. I filled the stove with whatever birch junks it could hold, and I opened the drafter. I barred the living-room door and directed Mae to sit in the draft of the porch door, warning her not to let on that she knew Jonas. By the time he yelled, 'Any mummers 'llowed in?', the stove was glowing red. 'Oh, 'tis a mummer, sure,' I said. 'Come in,' I said, and I led him to the rocking chair next to the stove.

"'Now that's a mummer I don't know,' I said. 'Do you know who it is, Mae?' Mae shook her head and pretended she was sizing up the mummer, looking fer clues. Well, I took my dead time and guessed my way through the place. 'Tis not Walt Churchill, is it?' I asked. 'Is it the schoolmaster? Thumb-On-Wrench Swyers?' And on and on I went.

"By and by I noticed him stretching out the top of his

long-johns and blowing down his neck. I knew my plan was working. 'Awful warm,' he said in his mummering voice. I kept right on guessing until I ran out of names. 'Must be someone from Kellop Harbour,' I said, and I started working my way through that place. Jonas was now squirmin' in the chair, and he was puffin' and blowin' and tuggin' at his costume.

"By the time I got about halfway through Kellop Harbour, he could stand it no longer. He jumped up and pulled the blanket from his head. His hair was soakin' wet and matted to his head. His face was blood red and the sweat was rollin' down his neck.

"'Well, goodness me, sure 'tis Jonas Pickett,' I said. 'I didn't guess ya, Jonas, boy, but I'll have to give ye a drink anyway, I s'pose.' 'Not fer me,' said Jonas. 'Every stitch I got on is soakin' wet and I'm feelin' a bit queasy.' With that, he jumped up and took off through the door. He barely made it down over the bridge when he threw up in the snow. He threw off the blanket, jumped out of the long-johns, un-zipped his snow suit, and gave it to her across the ice out to Manuel's Point."

"So you think that's how Jonas caught pneumonia, do you?" I asked Uncle Mark.

"I know it was," he responded. "I heard that he told Dr. Templeman that he got sick after he had been mummering on Old Christmas Night. He said he sweated so much in Mark White's house that he got soakin' wet, and every stitch he had on froze solid as he was walkin' home."

"What was he like when you saw him today?" I asked.

"Very good today," said Uncle Mark. "But I tell you—he was some glad to get that drop of soup."

Uncle Mark White Goes Cod Jigging

Most people in Roaring Cove were hopping mad this past summer because the Government cut off the recreational cod fishery, while permitting the tourists to continue to jig. None were as mad as Uncle Mark White; he was farting flankers.*

"They've taken away a God-given right," he said, "and I'll have me day fishin', no matter what." Well, Uncle Mark got his day fishing all right, and the story behind how he got it is well worth telling.

He called me and engaged a ride to Kellop Harbour for the next day. "Pick me up early," he requested, "and be prepared to stay for most of the day."

Bright and early the next morning, I pulled up in front of Uncle Mark's house. No sooner had I stopped the car than this strange-looking creature bolted out the door, scrabbled through the gate, and hopped in the front seat next to me. Upon closer inspection, I recognized this weird-looking individual to be none other than Uncle Mark White himself. He was wearing a straw hat, sunglasses, a brightly-coloured flower-imprinted shirt, short pants, and a pair of old sandals

---

* Live sparks, as from a wood fire.

that I recognized as belonging to Aunt Mae. I held my laughter until he settled in the seat and I got a good look at his bare, white, spindly legs. They somewhat resembled flake longers* that had been freshly whitewashed.

"Stop yer laughin' and drive," he demanded. We were halfway up Bakeapple Marsh Road before I got out of him what he was up to. "I'm goin' fishin'," he said. "There's a feller from the mainland that got Skipper Ned Macdonald's long-liner bought and got a tour boat made out of her. They tells me he's makin' a fortune takin' the tourists out cod jiggin'. Now, I'm not from Kellop Harbour—I'm from Roarin' Cove. So, the way I got it sized up, that makes me a tourist."

I had never seen so many people in Kellop Harbour. Sure, we had to line up all the way back to the post office to get to the government wharf.

"Now," said Uncle Mark, "I'll give ya the money fer yer ticket and you come on board, too, but don't let on that ya knows me."

Once on board, Uncle Mark quickly lost himself in the crowd of tourists, but he was the first one in line when the jiggers were handed out. I had to stand back and watch; I was only a Newfoundlander.

Well, what a commotion—there were jiggers going everywhere. One landed on the deck but inches from my foot, and one man had his cowboy hat hooked off and sent to the bottom on the top of a cod jigger. The commotion continued for the longest time and not one fish was landed. By and by,

---

* Flakes are elevated platforms used for drying fish. Flake longers are round, rough poles used to construct the surface of the flakes

Uncle Mark sneaked up behind me. "Go tell that bloody fool operator that we'll never jig a fish here—we're nowhere near the fishin' grounds."

"You tell him," I mumbled.

"I can't," he said. "I'm supposed to be a tourist; I'm not supposed to know where the grounds is at."

By this time, I was feeling a little bit like I had salt rubbed into a sore, and I was a small bit cantankerous. "I'm damned if I will," I said, "I hope they never catch a fish."

Uncle Mark sputtered something under his breath and went back to his jigging. Not long after, he struck one, and he professionally began pulling it in with a smooth, rhythmical hand-over-hand movement. "I got one on!" he yelled in a put-on accent.

Almost immediately, a tourist fishing next to Uncle Mark shouted in a thick brogue, "By golly, I believe I've hooked one, as well!"

"They must be strikin' on," said Uncle Mark, "and a fine big one I got on, too, by the weight of en."

"Well, mine must be but a wee tiny one," said the tourist. "My line is floating to the surface; the fish must be swimming up with it."

Uncle Mark took one look at the other man's line, and he knew exactly what was happening. "You're gone across my line and I got yer jigger hooked."

"Oh, you won't be tellin' me that, my man—'tis a fish I have on my line."

"No, the fish is on my line," Uncle Mark stated.

"So, you're tryin' to take my fish now, are ya?"

Uncle Mark stopped pulling in his line and came face to face with the tourist, ready to argue the point. As he did, the weight of the fish went on the other man's line.

"Ha, ha!" shouted the tourist. "Now I can feel the weight of my fish!" And he awkwardly began pulling it in.

Uncle Mark again grabbed his line and raced to regain the weight of the fish. The two men were now in a heated argument as they pulled frantically on their lines. "Well," I thought, "there's going to be a fuss here today." I knew Uncle Mark well enough to know that he wasn't about to back away from a racket when he knew he was right, so I hurried over to intercede. As I pushed in between the two, the fish broke the water, and it was hanging on the end of Uncle Mark's jigger. It was a big, old sculpin,* about three feet long.

"Oh, look at the size of the cod fish I've caught," announced the tourist.

"Well," responded Uncle Mark, "it happens that it is on my jigger, but that's all right, my son. You can have the fish—I was only tormentin' ya all the time."

---

* A thorny, scavenger fish with a large head and mouth — a curse to a fisherman fishing with hook and line.

Uncle Mark White's Rat

If you visit Roaring Cove and look down behind the post office in the town council compound, there barred in behind a chain-linked fence, you will see Uncle Mark White's rat—the pride of the whole town and the envy of all the other places up and down the coast. You see, Uncle Mark's rat is quite out of the ordinary; it is much larger than others of its kind and it has a different and unique shape. It came all the way from Texas, and the story of how it ended up in Roaring Cove is an unusual one indeed.

It all started one day in late June last summer when Uncle Mark and I went to Middleville to pick up a few supplies for a garden party that our newly-formed volunteer fire department was having to raise money to purchase a new fire truck. By lunchtime, the back seat of my car was full of paper plates, plastic forks and knives, admission tickets, stuffed animals, and other garden party odds and ends.

Our shopping was complete, so we went to the restaurant up on the highway to get a bite to eat before heading back to Roaring Cove. We ordered the special of the day and were waiting for it to be served when we heard this thunderous roar coming from outside. Through the front window, I saw fifteen or twenty motorcycles pulling into the parking lot. They ceremoniously circled several times, as if announcing their arrival, and parked in a neat row in front of the restaurant. The drivers dismounted, removed their helmets and sunglasses, and inspected their bikes. They congregated in the middle of the parking lot, held a brief discussion, and headed in single file towards the restaurant. Four or five people sitting near the back of the restaurant made a hurried exit through the side door.

"Maybe we should get out of here," I said to Uncle Mark. "I've read about motorcycle gangs like this. There could be trouble." I noticed a gleam in Uncle Mark's eye, and I realized that my comment had only fanned his lust for adventure.

"I fought the Battle of the Dardanelles, my son," he said. "I'm not afraid of a crowd the like a dat." He sat straight in his chair, ignored the meal that had been placed before him, and sized up the bikers as they entered the restaurant.

Around Middleville, they were a strange-looking crowd indeed. Most of the men wore long hair and beards of all shapes and styles. A couple had no hair at all, their heads having been completely shaved. There were only a few women. Their hair was held in place with handkerchiefs that were twisted across their foreheads and tied at the back. All faces were deeply tanned, and they looked as if a good bath would not have been wasted.

Both men and women were dressed identically, in black leather pants and jackets with high-heeled cowboy boots. Their outfits were decorated with silver studs that bordered the waistband and pockets of the pants and short pieces of chain that looped from the shoulder straps of the jackets. On the back of each jacket was a large yellow star. The words "Freedom Riders" were printed in red letters around the outside of the star, and in its centre was a symbol that resembled something between a set of bull's horns and a pitchfork.

These were not young people. Most of the beards were streaked with grey and the long hair was thin and wispy. I figured most of the people to be middle-aged at best.

They were noisy as they entered the restaurant, and they spoke loudly in slow, drawn accents.

"Queer lookin' crowd," Uncle Mark commented as he inserted his fingers into his soup bowl and extracted a salt meat bone which he immediately proceeded to strip of meat. He continued his assault on his dinner and his attention was fully taken up with his favourite pastime—eating. But, as he was waiting for his apple pie to be served, he noticed a bit of a show from one of the tables at which the bikers were sitting.

"Look there!" Uncle Mark said in a voice clearly audible to the three bikers at the table closest to us. "Buddy got a rat with en." He pointed his finger directly at the big, bearded man sitting at the head of the table.

My heart jumped into my throat, and I looked towards the man for some sort of a reaction. Much to my relief, the man's attention was focused on his huge hand that was outstretched over the table. A tiny hamster was running around his palm and in and out between his fingers. The man had removed his leather jacket; underneath he wore a denim shirt with the sleeves cut out. The little hamster ran over the bulging muscles of the man's tattooed arm and disappeared into his thick, bushy beard. It surfaced on the man's sideburns, climbed onto his head, and ran around and around.

The very amused Uncle Mark clapped his hands and laughed loudly.

Finally, the hamster ran down the man's neck and inside his shirt collar. Uncle Mark leaned forward in his chair and stretched his neck, searching for the little rodent.

"Dere he is! Dere he is!" Uncle Mark shouted excitedly,

pointing to the hamster surfacing from the front of the man's shirt. It jumped onto the table and ran wildly, sliding and slipping on the smooth tabletop. Uncle Mark again clapped his hands and laughed, making a snorting noise as he drew in his breath. When the animal began sniffing at the sugar dispenser, the big biker scooped his hamster friend into his hand.

Before I knew what was happening, Uncle Mark was off his chair and was hopping over to the man holding the hamster. "Show Uncle Mark yer rat," he half stated and half demanded. The big man stared ahead expressionless and silently. "Come on, show Uncle Mark. Uncle Mark's not gonna hurt yer bloody old rat."

The biker raised his foot and kicked out the empty chair from the table. "Sit down," he said. As Uncle Mark squatted in the chair, the biker handed him the hamster. Uncle Mark cupped his hands and received the creature. He stroked and petted it as he engaged in conversation with the three men.

I could not hear what was being said, but it was evident that Uncle Mark was doing most of the talking. It was also evident that these strangers were not offended by Uncle Mark's intrusion because they were smiling and, on a couple of occasions, laughed loudly. Then I noticed Uncle Mark lift his shirt and show the men his bare back. I knew they were getting the full details of his active war duty, so I figured it was time for us to leave.

"Excuse me, Uncle Mark," I said as I approached the table, "are you ready to leave?"

"Come here," he said, "and meet these fellers." He introduced me to Joe, Sid, and the big man, Hank. "And this little rat here is called a 'amster," he announced, holding the pet out in his hand. "Cute little feller, en he?"

I shook hands with the three men and made small talk with them as Uncle Mark gathered his cap and coat. He placed his cap on his head and gave it that distinguished little tip forward before returning to the bikers' table. We said our good-byes and were prepared to leave. I was holding the door for Uncle Mark when he suddenly turned back to the men. "You know what?" he said. "We're havin' a garden party in Roarin' Cove on Friday. All you fellers should come down to it; I guarantee a good time." I made my exit into the parking lot.

Uncle Mark's face was beaming with a broad smile when he got into my car. "They're comin' down to the garden party on Friday," he announced proudly.

"I wouldn't count on it," I said.

Around noon on Thursday, children lined the sides of the roads, old men leaned over the fences, and faces appeared in kitchen windows as a convoy of motorcycles invaded out little town. Like ants scurrying in their trails, the bikes wound their way along the narrow dirt road as the children chased behind. Revving the motors to echo the noise off the cliffs, the bikers drove to the end of the community, where the road meets a solid rock face. They stopped their bikes and got off. Some climbed up the cliff and looked out over the harbour; others threw stones from the road in an unsuccessful attempt to reach the water; a couple of men urinated over the edge of the cliff. Every move was carefully watched by all who lived below Sam Whiffen's shop.

Uncle Mark was on the road, waiting for them when they came back. It was Hank who pulled up alongside him. The first thing he did was to reach inside his jacket, pull out the hamster, and hand it to Uncle Mark. Uncle Mark held the hamster as he directed the bikers to what he calls "my big garden."

Uncle Mark's garden was a long, narrow, grassy field that was across the road from his house, down over the cliff, near the water. He used it years ago to grow hay and graze his animals. Today, it is only used by youngsters to play a scattered game of cricket and rounders.

The bikes slowly snaked their way down the steep footpath, and the big garden was soon transformed into a campground as bright orange pup tents blazed in the green grass, and smoke from the camp-stoves climbed lazily up the face of the cliff.

By four o'clock, Sam Whiffen's shop was completely sold out of beer, and concern ran through the community. Uncle Mark's telephone rang continuously. "They're on your property, so you'll be held responsible," Thumb-On-Wrench Swyers, Roaring Cove's mayor, said before Uncle Mark could hang up on him.

The first night was noisy. The bikers hooted and hollered and burned fires on the beach for most of the night. The next morning, Toby Avery's lobster vat was empty—twenty-two lobsters stolen. Toby pointed the finger of blame at the bikers. A public meeting was called, and all the toilets on the beach—the ones the bikers were using—ended up with padlocks on the doors.

The big concern at the meeting was the possibility of trouble at the garden party that night. Thumb-On-Wrench suggested that the party be postponed until after the bikers left. Uncle Mark stood up, buried his hands deep in his pockets, and said his piece, "I think you fellers are a bit quick to hang the cat. I thought the idea of havin' a garden party was to raise money for a fire truck, so I figured the more who attended the better—that's why I invited them fellers along. And besides, they seem like an all right bunch to me. We got no proof that it was they who stole Toby's lobsters—we've had lobsters stolen in Roarin' Cove before. And, as for puttin' padlocks on the toilets on the beach, I've had a toilet down there fer fifty year, and I haven't had anything stole out of it yet. And I don't suspect the bikers will steal anything from it now."

Well, most saw Uncle Mark's point, and the garden party went off as planned—and without trouble. As a matter of fact, it was the most successful and enjoyable garden party ever held in Roaring Cove, and it was the bikers who helped make it so. They arrived early in the evening and remained until a hint of orange sunshine glowed in the sky. They virtually bought out the concessions, and the beer tent turned in remarkable profits. They proved to be polite and friendly, and they socialized easily with the Roaring Covers. By the time the dance started, friendships were blooming, and plaid and leather blended well together. And once things got going, it was realized that the bikers and the Roaring Covers had something in common—they knew how to have a good time.

The floor of the old Fisherman's Hall was put to the ultimate test as it creaked and groaned under the assault of hundreds of dancing feet. The strangers were taught to dance the Roaring Cove jiggs, but they proved that they could cut a square set as well as anyone. When Paddy Whalen's fingers got sore from playing the button accordion, one of the bikers produced a concertina and picked up where Paddy had left off. A little later in the evening, one of the biker women played her guitar and sang in a voice that would have sweetened a pickle. Paddy and the concertina player joined in with her, and tired feet were rested as the dancing gave way to a sing-along.

Sometime during the evening, Art Pearce went up to Toby Avery and asked if forty-five dollars was enough to cover the lobsters. Toby had no idea what Art was talking about, but he played along and got the entire story out of Art. Apparently, on Thursday night, Art, Joe Stead and the devil-skin, Alfie Lambert were on a bit of a party up in Kellop Harbour. Sometime during the night, they figured that a good feed of lobsters was needed to add to the festivities. So, they came down to Roaring Cove and cleaned out Toby's vat.

The next day, Alfie, realizing that he was out of money and that the garden party was that night, lied to Art and Joe that Toby had found out that they had stolen his lobsters. Alfie then suggested that the proper thing to do was to pitch in fifteen dollars each and pay Toby. Of course, Alfie ended up with thirty dollars for the garden party.

When the sing-along was over, Thumb-On-Wrench Swyers went to the platform and called for attention. "Ladies and gentlemen," he said, "I have a couple of announcements to make. Before I do, however, as mayor of Roarin' Cove, I'd like to extend a warm welcome to our friends camping out in Uncle Mark's big garden, and I'd like to thank them for attending our garden party here this evening. Now, first, I'd like to announce that Toby Avery has found his lobsters. Secondly, I'm happy to announce that this evening we've raised a grand total of $2,234.22. I know we'll need many more fund-raisers before we can get our fire truck, but it is a good start."

While Thumb-On-Wrench was being applauded, the bikers congregated on the dance floor, and I noticed a motor-cycle helmet being handed around and bills being dropped into it. It was Hank who dumped the contents of the helmet in front of Thumb-On-Wrench. He and Walt Churchill began counting. "Another $235.00!" Walt shouted. The applause was long and sustained. A perfect ending to a perfect night.

The next morning, the padlocks were removed from the outhouses on the beach, and Toby Avery gave his entire morning catch of lobsters to the bikers as an apology for wrongly accusing them. Aunt Mae White baked bread, while Uncle Mark carefully packed the entire batch into the wheelbarrow and delivered it to the campsite, in time to go along with the lobsters. Hank fitted Uncle Mark with a leather jacket and a helmet and gave him a thrilling motorcycle ride halfway to Middleville and back. Other bikers gave the children rides through the community.

On Sunday morning, the last three pews of the church were full of leather. That afternoon, old men leaned on their fences and waved good-bye; smiling faces disappeared from kitchen windows, to reappear in doorways, with more waving; and the children chased the bikes all the way to Bakeapple Marsh Road intersection. No one in Roaring Cove ever expected to see or hear from the bikers again—but Roaring Cove was in for bit of a surprise.

Summer had faded into fall and the Christmas season was quickly upon us. It was a still Saturday morning and everyone was busy, stringing outdoor lights around almost anything that would support them. Suddenly, the screeching sound of a siren echoed through the community. Everyone thought it was the Middleville Santa Claus parade being led by a police car, and they lined the sides of the road to see it.

I was in Uncle Mark's shed, watching him shape out a model dory. The two of us went outside, leaned over his fence, and waited for the parade to come along. We looked at each other with surprise when a large lime-green fire truck rounded the corner and rolled down the road towards us. It pulled up in front of Uncle Mark's gate. His jaw fell open and he turned a pasty white when I read aloud the words printed on the side of the truck, "PRESENTED TO THE TOWN OF ROARING COVE, FROM THE TEXAS FRONTIER OIL COMPANY—AND THE FREEDOM RIDERS."

Two unfamiliar men stepped out of the truck and, in a deep southern drawl, requested "to speak with Mr. Mark White." Uncle Mark proudly presented himself and shook hands with the two men. "This is for you," one of them said, handing Uncle Mark a rectangular shaped object covered in a leather case. Surprised and unsure of how to behave or respond, he took the object and removed the cover. It was a wire cage. Inside, a small hamster ran wildly on a treadmill, and fastened to the outside of the cage was a silver name plate with the word "RAT" engraved on it.

The two men were promptly invited inside, and Aunt Mae prepared a lunch. The men told their story. They were employees of the Texas Frontier Oil Company of which Hank, the biker, was owner and president. With several oil fields and as many refineries, fire trucks were standard safety equipment for Hank's company. The truck the two had driven from Texas to Roaring Cove was one that was being replaced with a newer, more modern one. Hank, also the president of the Freedom Riders Motorcycle Club, decided that the replaced truck would make an appropriate gift for Roaring Cove.

A public meeting was quickly called and a very astonished Mayor Thumb-On-Wrench Swyers was presented with the keys to Roaring Cove's first fire truck.

The story of the fire truck went through the community

like a west wind, and by the time it reached Jonas Pickett on Manuel's Point, it was somewhat distorted and blown out of proportion. Old Jonas hurried in the harbour to see the big rat that had been given to Uncle Mark. He had heard it was so large that it had to be barred in the town council compound.

Well, that was it—the truck had acquired its name, and a few days later Thumb-On-Wrench put the truck in his garage and painted the words "Uncle Mark's Rat" in red letters along the front.

So, if you visit Roaring Cove and look down behind the post office in the town council compound behind the chain-linked fence, you will see Uncle Mark White's rat.

Jonas Pickett's Tooth

Jonas Pickett is the most notorious man in Roaring Cove. He has been called everything from a sleeveen to a miser, and Uncle Mark White says he is so crooked, he has to screw his stockings on in the morning.

A short while ago, old Jonas was forced to make a trip to Dr. Templeman's office, and he proved to everyone just what a conniving sort he really is. You see, dental hygiene is not one of Jonas' attributes and, for as long as anyone can remember, he has had a mouthful of very large, half decayed, tobacco-stained teeth. It was a toothache in two of his jaw teeth that caused him to visit Dr. Templeman and inquire into the cost of having them extracted. He was told it would cost $20 for the first tooth and $10 for the second one.

Jonas openly complained that the price was too high, and he stormed out of Dr. Templeman's. But the very next morning he was back—rampant with toothache. He instructed Dr. Templeman to pull his left jaw tooth. He said that he would have to put up with the pain in the right one until his pension cheque came.

The doctor went to work on Jonas and, after half an hour of tugging and prying, he extracted what he described as "the largest molar ever to come from a human mouth." He said that the roots of the thing somewhat resembled those of the big spruce tree that blew over Winse Hillard's new car during the big windstorm that fall.

Jonas was given the bill for $20.

"You've made a mistake on the bill," Jonas said through numbed lips.

"Oh, and why is that?" Dr. Templeman asked.

"You said it would only cost $10," Jonas answered.

"No, what I said was that it would cost $10 for the second tooth," Dr. Templeman explained.

"And, you just pulled the *second* tooth," Jonas said.

"I pulled only one tooth," the doctor said defensively, realizing that Jonas was scheming again.

"I know you pulled only one tooth," Jonas muttered, still clamping down on the packing that was filling the large crevice in his jaw. "But yesterday I showed you this *right* tooth and you said it would cost $20 to pull it. Then I showed you this *left* jaw tooth and you said it would cost $10 to pull it. Well, you just pulled that *left* jaw tooth, so 'tis simple—$10."

"Twenty," said Dr. Templeman.

"Well, as far as I am concerned, I was given misleading information," Jonas stated. "I've been cheated. If 'twas something I bought in the shop, I'd bring it back and get me money, but you can't very well give me the tooth back."

"Oh, yes I can!" declared the doctor, unwilling to let Jonas get one over on him. "You pay me the $20 you owe me, Jonas, or I'll put the tooth back in your head."

"Well, that's exactly what you'll have to do," Jonas said stubbornly.

Dr. Templeman sat Jonas in his special tooth-pulling chair and tended on several other patients until he was sure the anaesthetic was worn off and Jonas' jaws had come back to life. Then he took Jonas' tooth from the specimen bottle and showed it to him.

"It's going to be painful replanting these old roots, Jonas."

Jonas responded by opening his mouth.

Dr. Templeman removed the packing from Jonas' jaw, located an exposed nerve, and began to dig at it. Jonas' legs stiffened and tears welled up in his eyes. "I think it would be easier if you simply paid me the $20, Jonas," Dr. Templeman suggested.

Jonas shook his head, indicating the negative. It was now a game of bluff, and Dr. Templeman was not about to fold. He positioned Jonas' tooth above the hole from which it had come, and he pushed down hard. Jonas' body stiffened like a man jolted with an electric shock. He moaned and groaned and tried to get out of the chair, but the doctor had him pinned. Finally, Jonas squirmed his way down in the chair enough to squeeze his hand into his pocket. He pulled out a twenty dollar bill and waved it, signifying surrender.

Dr. Templeman politely took the money and marked the bill "Paid in full." Jonas said nothing; he left the office, holding his jaw with both hands.

Roaring Cove's Unusual Fire

Roaring Cove has had its new fire truck for over a year, and Hayward Green, the fire chief, and the volunteer fire department have not won the admiration of Uncle Mark White. He says they are like a bunch of youngsters with a new toy, and there have been several incidents that warrant him to hold such an opinion.

To begin with, on bonfire night Hayward took "rat", the fire truck, to the roads of Roaring Cove and patrolled back and forth on red hot alert. The children of Roaring Cove have been having bonfires for as long as anyone can remember, so Hayward's concern impressed few. And then, around 9:30 P.M. when the wind breezed up out of the northwest, he made a decision for the safety of all of Roaring Cove. The hoses were unrolled and every bonfire in the place was doused before the youngsters could even retrieve their baking potatoes.

On another occasion, Aunt Daisy Snelgrove had an untimely visit from Roaring Cove's noble fire department. Aunt Daisy was out in her front garden picking a few lilacs, and she began talking across the road to Jobie Rodgers who was out digging up a bit of potato ground. As usual, Aunt Daisy was complaining about not feeling well. She bawled out to

Jobie that her heartburn was so bad, she was afraid to burp for fear of setting fire to something. She was barely back in her house when the fire truck, with siren blaring, pulled up in front of her gate. Without warning, several men, heavily laden in rubber boots, were dragging a fire hose across Aunt Daisy's kitchen floor.

If this were not enough to rub Uncle Mark the wrong way, it was when he got his own visit from the fire truck, the truck that he takes credit for having brought to Roaring Cove, that put the kibosh on it. It happened in the middle of the night about a month ago. You see, Aunt Mae White's tomcat, Smokey, that she thought quite a bit about, had gone missing. Aunt Mae was very upset, but Uncle Mark told her there was nothing to worry about. He maintained that it was rutting time and Smokey was merely making his rounds and was probably easy enough about it.

Anyway, after the cat had been gone for a fortnight, Aunt Mae awoke one night to the sound of what she thought was a cat meowing. She awakened Uncle Mark and sent him outside to check it out. He went out on the back bridge and called out, "Here, Smoke ...Smoke...Smoke." It was a clear, still night, and the words "Smoke...Smoke ...Smoke" echoed back at him from the Roaring Cove cliffs. Within minutes, the fire truck and a string of cars were racing towards Uncle Mark's house. Uncle Mark said he was more embarrassed than at any other time in his life.

Consequently, when Hayward Green himself later suffered the embarrassment of having a fire on his property, Uncle Mark felt no sympathy for him. For the fire chief to have accidentally caused a fire was embarrassment enough, but the fire that Hayward caused was not your ordinary fire—Fire Chief Green had the most unusual fire ever seen in Roaring Cove (and perhaps anywhere, for that matter).

It was one of the coldest days we had this winter, and about ten o'clock in the morning, the fire truck went screeching past the schoolhouse. I looked out through the window and saw black smoke towering into the frosty air. "This is a real fire," I thought. "It should give the fire department a bit of excitement." But upon closer inspection, I noticed that the smoke was coming from Hayward's house. I went out on the schoolhouse bridge to get a better look and was there only a few minutes when I saw the fire truck returning. Thumb-On-Wrench Swyers was driving, which I thought strange because Hayward never let anyone else but himself drive the fire truck. I figured that Hayward was probably burning some old tires or something else as a training exercise for the other firemen. I thought nothing else about the matter until I went home for lunch.

I was barely in the house when I saw Uncle Mark coming through the gate. He was grinning from ear to ear and it was easy to see that he was delighted about something. "Did ya hear what happened to the big shot today?" he questioned.

"Who?" I asked.

"Mr. Fire Chief Green," he answered.

"Well, I saw smoke coming from what looked like Hayward's place this morning," I commented.

"Yes," said Uncle Mark, clapping his hands and laughing loudly. "Sure, this morning, Mr. Fire Chief went and burned down his own well!"

"His well?" I asked in disbelief. "How in the world can you burn down a well?"

"Easy, if you're the Fire Chief," Uncle Mark answered, not attempting to hide his sarcasm. "You see, Hayward's water-line froze last night, down in the well. Hayward came up with the bright idea of puttin' a propane heater down there in an attempt to thaw it out. The heater caught the plastic well liner afire, and Hayward didn't know what to do. He had no water in his house, so he grabbed a bucket, took off fer the landwash, and started dippin' up salt water."

"What about the fire truck?" I asked.

Uncle Mark was laughing so much he could hardly finish telling me the story. "He forgot about the fire truck until Peter Spurrell came running over and suggested it," Uncle Mark said. "By the time they got hold of Thumb-On-Wrench and he got there with the truck, the liner had burned out and Hayward's well had collapsed. Now, whatta ya think of that fer a Fire Chief?" As he finished speaking, Uncle Mark wiped tears from his eyes.

"Well, well, well," I commented.

My Trip to the Doctor

Seldom do I go to see Dr. Templeman, and when I do, it seems as if I always see or hear something to give me a chuckle. For example, one night earlier this winter, I stopped by the clinic to get something for a 'flu I had been playing host to for several weeks, and who should be in the waiting room but Sam Whiffen, Roaring Cove's fish merchant, businessman and most prominent citizen. Sam had a door knob sticking out of his gob*—yes, an antique brass door knob. The inner workings of the lock and dead bolt were still attached and were hanging over Sam's chin.

It was easy to see that he was embarrassed because he turned a crimson red when he saw me. He couldn't speak, so he greeted me by lifting the forefinger of his left hand. He was using his right hand to support the weight of the door knob.

I was curious about this strange predicament of Sam's, and I casually mentioned to Dr. Templeman that I had seen Sam Whiffen in the waiting room. I was hoping he would volunteer some information, but he simply smiled to himself and said nothing. I had to wait until the next evening before I got the story from Uncle Mark White. He had been down to

---

* Mouth.

Thumb-On-Wrench Swyers' garage and gotten all the details.

Apparently, Sam's shop had been broken into several times this winter. He suspected that it was a couple of young fellows from Kellop Harbour who had been seen hanging around, so he alerted the Mounties and requested that they keep a watch on his shop.

On this particular evening, Sam returned to his shop immediately after supper to do a bit of book work, as he did on evenings when the store was closed. When he tried the key in the door, he found that the lock was frozen solid. Without giving it a second thought, he knelt down on the step and began blowing into the keyhole in the hope that his warm breath would thaw the lock. Without warning, his lips and tongue stuck fast to the door knob. Try as he might, he couldn't free himself and, to make matters worse, he was at the office door at the back of the building, so there was little chance of anyone seeing him. His biggest fear was that he would freeze to death.

After about an hour, the Mounties drove by and, as requested, made a routine check of Sam's shop. They noticed a fresh set of tire tracks going around to the back of the building, so they stopped to investigate. They got out of the squad car, quietly circled the shop, and peeped around the corner. Sure enough, someone was picking the lock! They would catch the culprit in action, they thought. One Mountie stayed put while the other one crept down through the woods and came up behind. When in position, he sprang out, grabbed the would-be thief, and pulled him away from the door.

Sam's lips stretched out like a set of elastic suspenders until they could stretch no more. His head snapped back at the door, and he flattened his nose onto his face. Blood poured from his nose, ran down over the doorknob, and instantly froze, sticking Sam even more securely to the door.

By this time, the second Mountie was on the scene with a flashlight and recognized the thief as none other than Sam Whiffen himself. Sam was moaning and groaning and stamping his feet on the wooden bridge. The two very embarrassed Mounties tried to free Sam, but nothing worked. Finally, they got a tool kit from the police car, pried the door open, and unscrewed the doorknob from the inside. They took Sam to the doctor, the door hardware still attached.

"That's how he was when I saw him," I told Uncle Mark after he had told me the story.

Uncle Mark was not overly fond of Sam Whiffen; they had fallen out many years back over some fish that Uncle Mark claimed was culled in Sam's favour. "Too bad you didn't have the key," Uncle Mark said. "You could've locked shut that big mouth of Sam's forever."

Our Trip Upalong

It was a brilliantly sunny morning in Roaring Cove. A soft southwest wind from off the water gave the air a salty scent that caused Winse Hillard to instinctively drop his suitcase and look out over the sea. "Some morning out in the boat," he said in mild protest.

Before I could respond, Elsie, Winse's wife, burst through the door, reminding us that we had a ferry to catch in exactly ten hours, and that time had to be allotted for fog, car trouble and flat tires.

We were on our way to Toronto. My wife and I, along with Elsie and Winse Hillard, our closest friends in Roaring Cove, were on our way to the big city to attend Toby Avery's young fellow's wedding. Toby Jr. had moved to Toronto immediately after high school, landed a good job, and was about to marry himself a mainland girl. He sent everyone in Roaring Cove an invitation to the wedding.

Winse and Elsie were at our house one evening for a game of cards, and Elsie came up with the bright idea that we should take a summer holiday and attend the wedding. I had a brother whom I had never visited living in Toronto, so I thought it was a splendid idea.

However, Winse suggested that we were off our heads. You see, Winse is the shyest man I have ever known, and to get him to go anywhere was always a task, but to get him to

Toronto took the three of us a solid month of hard persuasion. He came up with every plausible excuse: "The house has to be painted this summer," "The gardens will turn to weeds if not tended to," and "Sure, that's the best time for troutin'."

Elsie countered all Winse's arguments with the simple, "You're afraid to go, Winse—afraid you'll have to speak to someone strange."

I knew Elsie was right because I could clearly recall the very first time I had met Winse. I thought he wasn't speaking because he was vexed over the fright I gave him when I walked unannounced into his shed. That first meeting is a story in itself, and we often get a chuckle out of it.

I was in Roaring Cove only a few days when the lock on the schoolhouse door refused to work. Not that the schoolhouse needed to be locked, but I thought it best to get it fixed. I was told that Winse Hillard was the best handyman in Roaring Cove, and I was directed to him. Winse's house was easy to identify; it was—and still is—the best kept property in the entire place.

Elsie answered the door and immediately engaged in friendly information-seeking conversation. I explained my purpose and she pointed down over the cliff, to a shed on the beach. "Winse is down in the shed," she said. "I don't know what in the world he's up to, but you can go down if you like."

As I inched my way down the steep and narrow footpath, I noticed that the shed door was tightly shut, smoke was billowing from a funnel that jutted crazily from a tar-papered roof, and all the windows were steamed up. I raised my hand to knock on the door, but I caught myself. This was a shed; Newfoundlanders didn't rap on shed doors, so I pushed the door open and walked in.

Winse had his back to the door, and he was down on his knees, holding a spoon over the end of a plastic tube. The heat struck me in the face and I noticed that a forty-five-gallon drum stove was glowing red with heat. Atop of the home-made stove, a silver cylinder rocked furiously and emitted little puffs of steam from around its cover. The cover was bolted down with long brass screws that projected from the cylinder like the tentacles of a squid. A copper tube rose from the bolts, looped around a four-inch nail driven into the rough wall, and ran halfway across the shed to where it was curled into a coil and submerged into a bucket of water that rested on an overturned barrel. Somewhere inside the bucket, the copper tube was joined to a clear plastic one; it slithered out of the bucket like a transparent snake and crawled down the side of the barrel and into a large glass jar. Winse was sampling the crystal clear liquid that was drip-ping from the tube.

I had seen moonshine made before, and I knew exactly what he was doing. I felt a sense of embarrassment at having caught Winse in this illegal act. I thought about trying to sneak out unnoticed, but reasoned against it, so I coughed above the noise of the roaring fire and the rocking tank, and got his attention. Blood red from the heat, his face quickly drained of its colour when he turned and saw me, a complete stranger, standing there.

"Are you Winse Hillard?" I asked.

Stunned, he looked from me to the stove, to the bottle, and back to me again. "I'm boiling out that old tank!" he blurted out. "I'm steaming a few lobster laths." Then his eyes fell on the spoon he was holding in his hand, and he knew he had been caught. "I'm runnin' a drop of stuff," he confessed.

"But I don't sell it or nothin'; I only runs a drop every now and then fer meself—'tis no harm in it."

"I'm the new schoolteacher," I said. "I wonder if you could fix a lock for me." And then, in an attempt to make light of the situation we both found ourselves in, I pointed to the jar on the floor. "That looks like a good drop of stuff," I commented. "I wouldn't mind trying a drop of that when it's run."

Winse responded by lifting the cylinder from the stove and gesturing to the door. As we walked up the path, I attempted to make conversation, but received only polite "yes" and "no" responses to my comments and questions. When we reached his house, he said, "I'll meet you at the school." And he disappeared into his porch.

It took Winse only a few minutes to repair the lock, and he worked in complete and uncomfortable silence. I was convinced that I had offended him, and was feeling rather badly over it. Without giving any details, I mentioned to Uncle Mark White that I believed I had offended Winse Hillard. Uncle Mark said that Winse was not the type to be easily offended, but he was a man of very few words.

It was almost Christmas before I saw Winse again. Just before supper one Saturday afternoon, there was a weak rap on the door. It was Winse. When invited, he stepped into the outside porch, put his hand inside his parka, and presented me with an unlabelled bottle of crystal clear liquid.

"You said you'd like to try this, Sir," Winse said. "So here's a drop for Christmas for ya." I knew Uncle Mark was right and that this was a gesture of friendship, so I readily accepted the gift.

"Well, thank you," I said. "Now come in and we'll drink a toast together."

"No, Sir," he responded. "It isn't right to give a feller a drop of stuff and then turn around and drink it on him. Besides, Elsie said for you and your missus to drop over and visit after supper."

The smell of freshly-baked bread met us at the step of the Hillard house, and we were barely inside the door when Elsie presented us with a triple-bun loaf to take home with us. And thus began a perfect friendship as we spent the first of many delightful evenings together. Winse always left the talking to Elsie, but he was always good company. He usually had a supply of his own "stuff" for sampling—the only thing he ever drank. He drank no beer, wine or liquor of any other kind; if there was none of his own, he drank straight tea. When he came to my house for an evening, he usually brought a flask of his own with him.

Some evenings, after he had three or four drinks of his "shyness medicine," as he called it, he would get out his button accordion and sweeten the room with Irish and New-foundland tunes. Other times, he would jump to the floor and break into one of his famous tap dancing steps. You see, besides being known for his shyness, Winse also had a reputation for being the best tap dancer, not only in Roaring Cove, but in the whole Southwest Arm.

And now, we were off to Toronto together. I knew that Winse was still uneasy about taking the trip, but I figured that once we got on the way and began seeing new and different things, he would relax. I was wrong. By the time we cleared the Montreal traffic, Winse's eyebrows were pulled into deep furrows; he was making quick and jerky move-ments with his head, and his stare was blank and empty like a man looking inward as opposed to outward. I had only seen him wear this expression twice before—once when we were caught in a thick fog while turr[*] hunting out the bay, and once when Elsie had her gallbladder operation.

By the time we reached my brother's house in Toronto, Winse was fretting like a broody hen. He shied away from meeting anyone and he absolutely refused to go out anywhere. The crisis came on the day of the wedding. We were sitting at the breakfast table when Winse surprised everyone, Elsie included, with the announcement that he didn't think he would be going to the wedding.

"Oh, and why is that?" I asked.

"I don't know. I don't think I'd fit in...you know...all them strangers...big shots," he stammered.

I looked straight at Elsie. She spoke not a word but looked straight at Winse, spit her partial plate into her hand, and gestured for him to follow her into the living room. In five minutes she emerged and matter-of-factly announced, "He's going."

It was a mainland wedding, quite different from the ones we were used to in Roaring Cove. There were receiving lines, formal introductions, and speech upon speech. So, Winse was not the only one uncomfortable. To make matters worse, Toby Avery Sr. and Jr. were ecstatic that we were there, and Toby Jr. felt obligated to introduce us to every living soul in the room. By the time we retreated into the ballroom for the dance, Winse was more than ready to barricade himself. He selected the table at the far corner of the room, and he wedged himself in the corner so that he was protected by a wall on either side and by the table at the front. When the band started, conversation was impossible anyway, so

---

[*] Sea bird, also called Murre.

Winse relaxed a little, sat back, and listened to the music.

The band was of German origin and played bouncy, upbeat polka music—perfect for setting the mood, and once I even caught Winse tapping his foot to one of the tunes. "Would you like me to get you a drink, Winse?" I asked when I made a trip to the bar.

"Nope," he responded automatically.

I delivered my tray of drinks to the table, and I motioned for Winse to follow me to the restroom. Happy to escape the crowd, he willingly came along. Once inside, I put my hand into my inside pocket and presented him with an unlabelled bottle of crystal clear liquid that I had saved for this occasion. His eyes lit up and the furrows in his brow disappeared for the first time in over a week.

"Well, where in the name of goodness did you get it?" he asked. He whipped off the cap, threw back three or four good mouthfuls, and offered the bottle to me. "Here you are," he said. "Have a swig. Better than anything you can buy at the bar."

"No, thank you," I said. "It's not right to give a feller a drop of stuff and then turn around and drink it on him." Winse tipped the bottle back a couple more times before returning to the table. We were back to our seats only a few minutes when the band struck up their rendition of "I'se the B'y." The mixture of Newfie jig and homemade "stuff" was more than Winse could resist. He sprang from his chair like an acrobat off a springboard and, agile as a cat, he danced his way around the tables to the dance floor.

"Look!" said Elsie, with a smile on her face. "Look at the bloody fool now."

In good Newfoundland fashion, he wasted no time taking a partner. He found his spot, threw back his head, brought his elbows perpendicular to his body, and slapped his feet at the floor like a man stomping the life out of a venomous creature. In a matter of seconds, he had the floor to himself. People simply stood around him in a circle, clapped their hands, and urged him on. They had never seen the like before as Winse demonstrated why he held the undisputed title of Roaring Cove's best tap dancer.

This was not the professional tap dance that most people were used to. This was a Winse Hillard original with no special shoes, training and routine. He was a live wire as he danced to the clapping and cheering of his sophisticated audience. Heel and toe clicked the floor like the castanets of a flamenco dancer. Not one beat did he miss. What he did not hit off the floor, he hit with a hand-clap underneath his legs or by clicking both heels together. And then, when the crowd believed that there was nothing more this man could do with his body, his knees came together, his feet parted at right angles to his torso, and he collapsed—simultaneously he bounced both knees off the floor and was back on his feet without missing a beat. Winse dazzled those mainlanders with his best performance ever.

For the remainder of the night and into the wee hours of the morning, Winse was the life of the party. Every time he would set his course for the table, some woman would grab him and drag him back to the dance floor.

"Having a good time, Winse?" I asked as I danced my way up to him.

"The best, boy," he responded. "The best, thanks to the shyness medicine."

After the wedding, Winse relaxed and was more like himself for the rest of the trip. He left most of the talking to Elsie, but he was good company.

The Hypochondriac

A hypochondriac is a person who is abnormally concerned with his or her health, especially minor symptoms. At least, that's what the dictionary says it is. Well, in that case we have a hypochondriac living right here in Roaring Cove. Aunt Daisy Snelgrove fits the definition so well that they could take her picture and put it in the dictionary right alongside the meaning.

Aunt Daisy was born deaf on her left side, and it is my belief that this is what started her obsession with sickness. Dr. Templeman claims that Aunt Daisy has been to visit him more often than all the other people of Roaring Cove put together. And, since the new hospital opened in Middleville, Aunt Daisy's chart fills a complete drawer of a filing cabinet.

Well, Aunt Daisy's most recent ailment came the other day when she was bottling up a few beets that she had grown in her own garden, and she accidentally splashed boiling water over her hands. Her first reaction was to panic. She called in an emergency to Dr. Templeman, wrapped her hands in her apron, and ran screaming into his office, without waiting to be properly admitted.

It took the doctor only a few minutes to examine Aunt Daisy's burns and prescribe ointment, but it took him the best part of an hour to convince her that her arms didn't have to be amputated. Then, later in the night, when the sting went away, she convinced herself that infection had set in. She saw an urgent need to get a second opinion, so she made an appointment at the Middleville hospital for the next day. She called me and engaged a ride.

Aunt Daisy talked non-stop all the way from Roaring Cove to the hospital door. She gave me her complete medical history, from her deaf ear to her so-called women's problems. She told me about her rheumatism, bad heart, and varicose veins, and I got the complete details about the time her foot festered after she stepped on an osy-egg* needle and how she eventually drew it out with a bread poultice.

She was still talking as she was being called for her appointment. I settled myself in for a bit of a wait, but it was still early in the morning, so I figured that even with Aunt Daisy's talking to the doctor, I'd be home by lunchtime. I was wrong. Lunchtime came and went and there was still no sign of her, so I went to the nursing station and inquired. I was told that Aunt Daisy was undergoing a series of complicated blood tests, and that I was permitted to visit her.

I was led into a little room where Aunt Daisy was lying in a bed. She was hooked up to all sorts of contraptions and her face was a deathly white.

"What's going on, Aunt Daisy?" I asked.

"Oh, you had better go home, my son. I'm done fer. I'm bleeding internally and they can't find the cause of it."

"Well, how long has this been going on?" I asked. "When did you first notice it?"

"It started just now," she responded. "I noticed it myself.

---

* A sea urchin.

When I went to the bathroom in the examination room, I filled the toilet with blood."

I thought to myself that finally Aunt Daisy had something to be genuinely concerned about. And, I was concerned, too, so I tried to comfort her. "Don't you worry now, Aunt Daisy—'tis probably nothing at all to it. I'll stay around until they find out something."

I was expecting a long wait before I got the official word on Aunt Daisy, so I went to the cafeteria and had an overdue lunch. I was barely back to the waiting room, though, when the door burst open and out charged Aunt Daisy. Her face had regained all its colour and was blood red; her purse was tucked up underneath her arm, and she had a full head of steam on, heading for the outside door. I chased her into the parking lot, but I had to run to keep up with her.

We were well outside of Middleville before she told me what had happened, but she made me promise not to breathe a word of it to anyone.

"All the tests came back normal," she said. "The doctor informed me that he could find nothing out of the ordinary, and then he asked me if I had eaten anything unusual. Well, the minute he mentioned that, it struck me—the beets. I can eat a barrel of raw beet, you know, and as I was bottling up some yesterday, I must've eaten seven or eight. Right away, I knew what it was I had seen in the toilet. Now, then, you know I wasn't embarrassed; I could feel me colour coming and going. I wouldn't dare let on to the doctor, though, so I told him I had nothing unusual to eat. Then he said he had better check me blood pressure because me face was gone as red as a beet. 'There's nothing wrong with me blood pressure,' I told him, and I grabbed me clothes and got out of there as fast as I could."

Well, I was true to my word and didn't mention a thing about Aunt Daisy's beets to anyone—well, almost...I did tell Uncle Mark White.

Uncle Mark chuckled to himself and said, "Well, well. That beats all."

The Pop-Up Toaster

It was by far the nicest day we have had in Roaring Cove that summer. I awoke to watch the sun rise a crimson red over Roaring Cove's cliffs, and the harbour was a pool of quicksilver. I cursed the government as I looked at my little boat lamenting on her collar.* Uncle Mark White and I were geared up to get a few codfish to salt for the winter, but the government had declared a moratorium on the Newfoundland codfishery because of depleting stocks, and codfishing of any sort was strictly forbidden.

I knew Uncle Mark would also be up, admiring the morning, so I dodged down to his house. The smoke from his chimney was rising straight into the still air, and I could smell bacon frying as I entered his gate. "I thought Dr. Templeman warned you about eating too much fat," I teased as I entered the kitchen.

"The devil with Dr. Templeman, and the devil with the fat," he grunted. "The way I got it sized up, if it tastes good 'tis bad fer ya—so I eats it anyway."

It was easy to see that Uncle Mark was in a foul mood. "What a morning we missed on the water," I said, knowing

_____

* An anchor and buoy used to moor a boat.

full well that my comment would do nothing to improve his disposition.

"Yes, the bloody government should be strung up," Uncle Mark said. "They've made a mess of the fishery, me son—a bloody mess—and I doubt if I'll ever be 'llowed to jig another cod."

As Uncle Mark was sputtering, I watched him open the bread box, take out a loaf of homemade bread, and cut off two thick slices. He hobbled across the kitchen to the garbage can, lifted the cover, and threw in one of the slices. The other one he put in the toaster.

"Uncle Mark, are you feeling all right?" I asked. "Do you realize that you just threw a perfectly good slice of bread in the garbage?"

"Of course I do," he responded. "I might as well—ever since Mae got that new-fangled, pop-up toaster, I always manages to burn up the first slice anyway."

"Well, isn't it working properly?" I asked.

"Oh, 'tis working the best kind—'tis not that. The trouble is, the thing is too modern. It's only made for baker's bread; the homemade stuff gets stuck in it." He picked up the bread knife and gave the toaster three or four taps. "And that's why we're not out fishin' this morning, because of the like of this," he continued.

"We're not out fishing because of the toaster?" I asked in a tone of confusion.

"Well, not the toaster exactly," he explained, "but because of stuff like it—you know, modern stuff. It's the modern stuff that destroyed the fishery, me son."

"I suppose," I said.

"No s'posin' about it," he said. "That's the way it is. You take, for instance, in years gone by, if a feller wanted to make a bit of toast, he put the grate over the hot coals, and he watched over it one slice at a time. Nothing got wasted or thrown away. Today, it's pop it in three or four slices at a time, turn your back to it, and do something else, hoping that a machine can tell the difference between a baker's slice and a homemade slice. Well, it can't—no more than a dragger hauling a net over the bottom can tell the difference between a small fish and a big one, or from a codfish and a turbot." Uncle Mark was wound up, and he continued, "Now, everyone lays the blame on the foreigners. But it was more than the foreigners who had a hand in destroyin' the fish. 'Twas no foreigner who brought that toaster in this house." He paused slightly and rubbed his chin. "Just the same," he said, "it was printed on the box that it was made in Japan."

With that, I looked over Uncle Mark's shoulder and I saw smoke towering from the toaster. "Your toast is afire, Uncle Mark!" I yelled.

Uncle Mark scrabbled over to the counter and whipped the plug from the wall. With the bread knife, he pried a slice of coal black bread from the toaster. "Another one wasted," he said, throwing this slice in the garbage, alongside the other. "If I don't give this up, Mae is going to declare a moratorium on homemade bread."

A Tribute to
Silas Murphy

Roaring Cove was greatly saddened this past week to learn
of the passing of one of its most colourful characters. Silas
Murphy, aged seventy-six years, passed peacefully away
from natural causes.

I went to the church last evening to see Silas and to pay
my last respects. As I gazed upon the waxen replica of Silas,
I noticed that he didn't look at all like himself. What was
different was that Silas looked peaceful and expressionless,
like any normal person who had been laid to rest. You see,
Silas was Roaring Cove's simpleton; greatly loved he was,
but normal he wasn't.

Slias was best known for his ability to fabricate and
exaggerate stories, and what was unique about him was that
he believed every word of his exaggerations. He was quite
convincing, for example, when he would proudly proclaim
that he was the owner of the fastest car in Roaring Cove, a
1962 Ford Pontiac, with twelve wheels, a 3,000-horsepower
motor, two steering wheels, and a brass compass that was
salvaged off the *Titanic*.

My first memory of Silas is synonymous with my first
day of teaching. I had arrived at the little schoolhouse sometime shortly after the birds began chirping and, to overcome

my nervousness, I entertained myself by observing the bubbling enthusiasm of the little ones and the sulking reluctance of their older brothers and sisters. I was watching a couple of senior boys enjoying the last few minutes of summer freedom by alternately puffing on a cigarette, when I noticed this adult stumbling up the road. My attention was immediately drawn to the spasmodic movement of this man's body and the sticks that he was using to support himself.

Although Silas was never diagnosed, he must have had some sort of spinal disorder because his back was extremely hunched and his legs were twisted and bowed. Consequently, he required the aid of two sticks in order to keep his balance. He never used regular walking canes, though, but instead used any old stick he could find. This day he was using a broken hockey stick handle and an old fence picket.

He came straight up the road with arms, legs and sticks swinging unproportionately, and into the school yard he turned. As he approached, I noticed two large, yellow teeth hanging over his bottom lip. Through these he grotesquely emitted a spray of spit as he sounded a guttural grunt each time his foot found the step ahead of him.

Silas' teeth were as much a part of his physique as was his twisted body. One or the other of his top two canines, the only two teeth he had left in the front, always protruded over his bottom lip, causing his top lip to curl in a perpetual smile.

Silas mounted the schoolhouse steps and greeted me. "Good morning, schoolmaster, I'm in the first grade," he said. He went inside the classroom and sat in the broken seat at the back of the room—the one with the pencil sharpener attached to it. I was too shocked to say anything; I just stood there and watched, my mind searching through my teacher training for a textbook plan of action. Before I could decide on one, a mature girl from the senior class noticed my distraught expression and came to my rescue.

"That's Silas Murphy, Sir," she said. "You don't have to worry about him; he's perfectly harmless. He comes on the first day of school every year, and he'll come every day at recess time, but he won't come inside again until the last day in June."

She was right. Silas sat in the seat and played with the pencil sharpener until recess time, then he left. This was Silas' routine; he had done the same thing each year long before I came to Roaring Cove, and has every year since—until now.

She was also right about Silas coming at recess time. Each recess break without fail, when it was fine enough for the children to play in the school yard, Silas showed up and entertained the children with his antics and stories. The children loved Silas as much as he loved the children.

Silas was also kind to the children. Every day before coming to the school yard, he stopped off at Sam Whiffen's shop and bought candy to share among them. It was this act of kindness that caused concern among some of the newer members of our community and, a short while ago, the matter got raised in a regular parent-teacher meeting.

The newcomers were the families that moved to Roaring Cove when the new fresh fish plant opened. They became known as "the higher-ups" because they held the management jobs and separated themselves from the rest of the community by building huge homes at the back of Roaring Cove Pond. They burned oil while everyone else burned wood, went to Middleville to do their shopping, and took long southern vacations.

Mrs. Dorothy Taylor was the spokesperson for the higher-ups. She was a small, thin woman with razor-sharp features and tiny, spindly legs that she accented by wearing extremely high-heeled shoes. She somewhat resembled a sandpiper that night she stood at the podium and announced in her proper accent that it was the opinion of the community that Silas Murphy was a threat to the children. "It's very wrong and suspicious for an adult person to buy the affection of young children with candy," she said.

Now, I understood the concerns because these people didn't know and understand Silas the way the rest of us did. I was therefore compelled to speak in Silas' defense. "Silas Murphy is a perfectly harmless individual whom the children adore," I told them.

"But it's not right for children to adore strangers," Mrs. Taylor retorted.

"Silas is hardly a stranger," I said, "and besides the children view him as another child—and really, mentally, that's all he is."

"But physically Mr. Murphy is very much an adult," she stated matter-of-factly.

"Silas is a warm sensitive person," I continued, "and those of us who know him well are convinced that your children are perfectly safe around him."

"Well, I happen to think you are wrong," said Mrs. Taylor. "I don't believe you know this man as well as you think you do because I have observed him standing on Roaring Cove Beach, directly in front of my windows, and undressing down to his underwear."

"And what did he do after he undressed?" I asked.

"He waded into the water and swam across the pond," she answered.

"Well, you didn't expect him to swim fully clothed, did you, Mrs. Taylor?" I asked, unsuccessfully trying to hide my sarcasm. I knew exactly why Silas was undressing on Roaring Cove Beach, and I related my story to the meeting in an attempt to explain Silas' behaviour and hopefully to gain a little sympathy for him.

Silas, you see, loved to swim. He was as awkward as a penguin on the land, but he was like a fish in the water. He often bragged about his swimming ability, and he often told the story about how he had survived the *Southern Cross* disaster. The *Southern Cross* was a Newfoundland sealing ship that disappeared in a savage spring storm on her return trip from the seal hunt in 1914. No trace of the ship or her crew was ever found. Silas had claimed that he was a crew member on the *Southern Cross*, and that he had swam ashore with a barrel of salt beef on his back and a bottle of rum in each back pocket.

Silas swam Roaring Cove Pond for the first time some twenty years ago on the day that his mother was buried. He swam to the far end of the pond to the swampy cove where the water is shallow and the grasses and pond lilies grow abundantly from the muddy bottom. He picked a large, yellow pond lily, held it in his mouth, and dog paddled back across the pond; the pond lily was placed on his mother's grave. Each year, on the anniversary of his mother's burial, he carried out the same ritual. This was no doubt what he was doing when Mrs. Taylor had seen him undressing on the beach, and I told her so. She was not convinced nor impressed, though; her feathers had been ruffled and she left the meeting, threatening to take the matter to higher authorities.

The matter went nowhere because it was only a couple of days later when two of Mrs. Taylor's younger children, a twin, and little Sally Baker, the fish plant manager's daughter, were playing on an old oil drum in Roaring Cove Pond. The drum floated away from the shore, became filled with water, and sank. The screams of the drowning children brought Mrs. Taylor up to her waist in Roaring Cove Pond, hysterically calling out for help. It was the middle of the day, so the men were at work and the women were doing whatever it is that higher-up women do in the middle of the day; consequently, her cries echoed off the Roaring Cove Cliffs unanswered. Unable to swim a stroke, hysteria caused her to run out the road towards the community. It was Friday, and Fridays were Silas' day to search the community for discarded beer bottles which he collected and sold to obtain money to buy candy for the children. Luckily, on this day he was searching the ditches on Roaring Cove Pond Road and was the first person Mrs. Taylor came upon.

Like a true hero, Silas answered the call. He tried following Mrs. Taylor up the road to where the children were, but he couldn't keep up. She tugged on him in an attempt to get him to move faster, but his feet became tangled in his sticks and he stumbled and fell. Realizing that he was wasting valuable time, Silas turned off the road and cut through the alder bushes to the side of the pond. From there, he could see the children. Without hesitation, he stripped to his underwear, in front of Mrs. Taylor, and took to the water. He wasted no time swimming; he dived, shot through the water like a torpedo, and surfaced well offshore. He released air, gasped air, and went down for the second time. His next dive took him to the children, and one by one he safely brought them to shore.

Silas was a hero, and no one knew it better than he. Somewhere, he had found some World War Two medals, and he proudly displayed them on his chest, claiming they had been personally pinned there by the Queen of England for saving one hundred children from drowning in Roaring Cove Pond. We heard nothing else about Silas Murphy being a threat to anyone.

I was dreading Monday morning in school because I knew the children would be upset over Silas' death. I tried carrying on with regular school work, but the students wanted to talk about Silas. I thought that the cleansing of emotions was healthy, so I permitted them to do so. There were tears and there was laughter as the students took turns telling stories that Silas had told them. There was the story about the time he killed the two hundred ducks with one shot, about the time he ate seventy-five eggs for breakfast, about his cat that could play the accordion and tap dance, and about the time he walked from France to Germany to have a game of cards with Hitler. Even Little Bobby Johnson, the shyest boy in school, wanted to contribute.

"I have a poem written about Silas," said Bobby in a low voice.

"Well, why don't you read it to the class?" I encouraged.

Much to my surprise, Bobby stood up, smoothed out his wrinkled paper, and began to read:

No survivors on the Southern Cross
Disappeared with all hands lost.
One hundred seventy-three men
Never to be heard from again.
But Roaring Covers all well knew
Silas Murphy was a part of her crew.
Swam ashore he stated as fact
A barrel of salt beef on his back
A bottle of rum in each back pocket
Now whoever would have thought it!

After Bobby had received a loud round of applause, Penny Green piped up with a suggestion that I had expected someone to make, "We should have a holiday, Sir—in remembrance of Silas." The rest of the class verbalized their approval for Penny's suggestion. I explained that I didn't have the authority to declare a holiday, but I promised to take them all to the church to pay their last respects to Silas. My condition was that, during the lunch break, they were to obtain written permission from their parents. I insisted on the written permission because I realized that this wasn't an ordinary school outing and some would probably have objections. Nevertheless, I personally felt that the experience was worthwhile. I felt that permitting the children to see a corpse would help remove some of the mystique of death.

After the lunch break, the permission slips were scattered over my desk, but a quick attendance check showed six students absent. All six were from the Roaring Cove Pond area—children of the higher-up families. I interpreted the absenteeism as non-approval of my church visit. I was somewhat disappointed, but not overly surprised.

In anticipation of their outing, the students were restless and inattentive, so I began our excursion earlier than planned. It was a bright and sunny afternoon in early June and we lazily strolled up to the church where Silas was resting. The children were silent and sombre and unsure of how to behave when I ushered them up through the church to Silas' open casket. In awesome silence, ten innocent souls stood around and stared at the body of their dead friend. Penny Green, as observant as always, whispered that Silas didn't look like himself. "He's not smiling, Sir," she said. "I've never seen Silas when he wasn't smiling."

I placed my fingers to my lips and was silencing Penny

when I noticed Chubby Charlie Freak fumbling through his pockets. I realized that it was mid-afternoon and it was snack time for Charlie. Before I could catch his attention to stop him, he pulled a full, intact cake of hard bread[*] from his trousers pocket. Simultaneously, ten dirt-grained hands were ceremoniously extended over the open casket. Looking around for an appropriate place on which to break the bread, Chubby Charlie's gaze fell on the glossy, protruding forehead of Silas. He cupped the cake in his hand and gave it a quick, hard knock that landed just above the bridge of Silas' nose. Without hesitation, the bread broke into a multitude of pieces. Charlie quickly gathered the offering and reverently distributed it into the cupped waiting hands. All pieces were hungrily devoured, except for one tiny crumb that had rolled into a crevice at the corner of Silas' mouth. Only too willing to share and share alike, Charlie, with forefinger and thumb, pried Silas' lips apart and, with his pinkie finger, flicked the last morsel into Silas' mouth.

Immediately, the other children began to snicker, so I decided it was time for us to leave. As I was escorting the children from the church, Chubby Charlie pointed to the casket. "Look, Sir," he said. "Silas is smiling again."

Apparently, Charlie's generosity had caused one of Silas' teeth to slip out over his bottom lip, causing him again to wear his familiar smile.

"Silas was happy to see us," Penny Green commented. "We made him smile again."

All the children looked back to see Silas smiling, and we left him as we had known him.

---

[*] Same as hard tack.

Once outside the church, I dismissed the children for the day, and I walked back to the schoolhouse alone. As I turned into the school yard, I recalled my first day of teaching so many years before, when Silas came into my classroom. I thought about how, over the years, I had come to celebrate the first and last days of school with his presence. I visualized him sitting in his special seat and I visualized him in the school yard distributing candy to the children, and I swallowed a lump that had risen in my throat. As I walked into the classroom, I felt a sense of accomplishment; I felt good about having brought the children to the church. In my heart, I somehow knew that Silas would have been pleased.

And then, I noticed the permission slips on my desk and I thought about the six higher-up children who hadn't shown up. I felt betrayed, and I felt as if they had betrayed Silas. But suddenly, in my peripheral vision, I caught a hint of colour. There, at the back of the room on the old seat with the pencil sharpener, were six large, yellow pond lilies. A wave of happiness swept over me. I picked a beaker from the shelf, filled it with water, and placed the lilies into it. Tomorrow I would place them on Silas' grave, but for now they would be placed in the window overlooking the school yard.

I whistled a tune as I exited the classroom, and I said aloud, "There lying upon Silas Murphy's desk were five hundred pond lilies."

Silas Murphy
Gets Arrested

Everyone in Roaring Cove knew that Silas Murphy loved to spin a yarn and greatly embellish it with exaggeration. Silas, the town's simpleton, was known and loved by everyone, and often his wild imagination was the source of much needed humour. Well, one night, his imagination didn't humour a young Mountie, and Silas ended up getting arrested because of it.

It was the first year that Alfie Lambert, Art Pearce and Joe Stead went to the mainland to work on the lake boats, and were home for the winter, enjoying the good life. On this particular night, the boys were engaged in their usual nightly entertainment, driving around Roaring Cove with an old guitar and an adequate supply of beer. Sometime during the evening, they saw Silas walking down the road, and they picked him up. Now, Silas never drank in his life; his role was to entertain the beer drinkers with his stories. And by all reports, he did a good job of it because Alfie was in a fit of laughter when he hit a spot of black ice on Bakeapple Marsh Road and left the car high and dry in a snowbank.

Realizing that the Mounties were on the prowl and that they had had more than enough to drink, the three buckos jumped out of the car, grabbed the remaining beer, and abandoned the scene. Silas was left in the car alone. He climbed into the front seat, slipped behind the steering wheel, and pretended he was driving. When the Mountie shone his light into the car, Silas was bouncing wildly in the seat, twisting the steering wheel like a race car driver, and was imitating the sound of the motor by vibrating his lips between his protruding front teeth. The Mountie, of course, didn't know but that Silas was the actual driver, so he asked to see his license and registration.

"Got no license," Silas said, "but I got a captain's ticket. Will that do?"

"Is this your car?" the Mountie asked.

"Yes, Sir, indeed it is," Silas responded. "A 1962 Ford Pontiac with a 3,000-horsepower, diesel motor—spent twelve springs to the ice in this baby, I did."

"What is your name, Sir?" the Mountie asked.

"Captain Silas Murphy."

"What happened for you to leave the road, Mr. Murphy?"

"Drivin' too fast."

"And exactly how fast were you driving, Mr. Murphy?"

"Five hundred miles an hour," Silas responded with a wink and a nod.

"Step out of the car, please, Mr. Murphy, and walk up to the police car."

Silas, who couldn't walk anywhere without the use of two sticks, reached into the back seat to get them, but the Mountie stopped him. Without this support, Silas stumbled and fell in an attempt to get up over the roadside.

"Have you been drinking?" the Mountie asked.

"Indeed I have," Silas proudly proclaimed.

"How much did you have to drink, Sir?"

"I had five bottles of rum and twenty-five dozen bottles of beer."

"I think you had better accompany me back to the station," the Mountie said, escorting Silas to the squad car. Silas, of course, was ecstatic over the idea of getting a ride in a police car, and once in the car he decided that he too was a RCMP officer. He quickly informed his new partner about the time he was shot fifty times while apprehending two bank robbers and about how he singlehandedly arrested two foreign draggers for overfishing.

When the Mountie went into the gas station in Middleville, Silas figured it was time to see what the police car could do. He jumped behind the steering wheel, put on the Mountie's cap that was left on the dash, and began playing with the steering wheel and flicking at switches. Suddenly, the red lights flashed on, and the siren screeched out over Middleville. Before the Mountie could get back to the car, Silas, pulling at the gear stick, knocked the car into neutral. It rolled down the grade, across the road, and through a picket fence, coming to rest on the lawn of Middleville's prestigious mayor.

Within minutes, the mayor and half of Middleville congregated to hear Silas explain to a very embarrassed police officer that he had lost control after the chain on the steering rudder broke.

The Squatting Stick

Last Saturday morning, Uncle Mark White and I strolled down to Thumb-On-Wrench Swyer's garage to catch up on a bit of news, as we do lots of Saturday mornings. Peter Spurrell, Gideon Forward and Ralph Sheppard, the fellows who always hung around the garage (the ones Uncle Mark called "the posse"), were there, and all the talk was about Roaring Cove's devilskin, Alfie Lambert. Thumb-On-Wrench was telling about the time he caught Alfie making his water down the government well.

"God only knows how many times he did that before I caught him," Thumb-On-Wrench said. "And the only explanation he gave for doing it was that he liked to hear his water trickling over the rocks, and he liked to see the steam rising from the well."

"He needs to be taught a good lesson before he hurts someone," added Peter Spurrell.

Now, I knew as well as anyone that Alfie was bad and mischievous, but I didn't believe for a second that he would deliberately hurt anyone, so I spoke up in his defense. "You know," I told the posse, "when Alfie was in school, he nearly drove me off my head. But since he graduated, there hasn't been one Christmas gone by that he doesn't come to visit me. I know he likes to drink, but he never takes one from me; he brings up something that happened back in school and we have a grand laugh over it."

"Yes," agreed Ralph Sheppard, "and last winter when I was in the hospital, it was Alfie who organized a collection for me. So, he can't be all that bad."

"What brought on all this about Alfie, anyway?" Uncle Mark asked.

"Didn't you hear what Alfie did to Jonas Pickett?" Gideon asked.

"No, but I can't imagine it being so bad that old Jonas didn't deserve it," Uncle Mark commented.

"He cut Jonas' squattin' stick almost in two, that's what," Thumb-On-Wrench said.

"What's a squatting stick?" I asked.

"A stick you sit on when you use the toilet outside," Uncle Mark answered in a tone that told me I should have known.

"You know Jonas' old toilet down in the beach, the one he inherited when he bought the house from Tacker Manuel fifty-odd year ago," Thumb-On-Wrench continued. "Well, Jonas has been using that same old toilet ever since. The seat and everything have rotted away, and of course Jonas was too lazy to build a new one, so he simply nailed a stick between the two walls and squatted on it whenever he used the toilet."

"That's a squattin' stick," Gideon interrupted.

"Be quiet, Gid, and let me finish me story," Thumb-On-Wrench snapped.

It was Thumb-On-Wrench's garage, so he got to tell the stories or offer a bit of gossip first. He continued, "Anyway, the devilskin, Mr. Alfie, was down along the shore with the gun the other day, lookin' fer a salt water duck. On his way back, he was short taken and made an emergency visit to Jonas' toilet. Of course, when he saw the squattin' stick Jonas had rigged up, his devious mind began to scheme. There was nothing for him to do but to return later that night with a handsaw and, from the bottom, cut through the stick to within an inch of the top. The next morning, as large as life, Jonas marched down to the toilet to do a job, and pounced down on the squattin' stick. The stick broke off and Jonas ended up down in the hole on the broad of his back."

"Did he hurt himself?" Uncle Mark asked with a smirk.

"No," answered Gideon, interrupting again. "The pile of stuff broke the fall, but 'tis a wonder he didn't suffocate. He was down there for over two hours and would be down there yet, I s'pose, if a couple of young fellers going down around the shore didn't hear him bawlin' out."

Jonas Pickett Takes His Turn as Church Sexton

It has always been the practice here in Roaring Cove for every able-bodied man to take a turn as church sexton. The sexton's job is to ring the church bell, take up the collection, tend to the furnace, and shovel the snow off the steps. Up to last month, Jonas Pickett, Roaring Cove's sleeveen, was the only man who had never taken a turn. Every year, the Reverend King put Jonas' name on the list, and every year, Jonas came up with some kind of excuse as to why he couldn't do it.

Well, again this year, the Reverend King signed up Jonas for February and, sure enough, immediately after Christmas, Jonas sent a letter to the minister, explaining that he couldn't take his turn as church sexton because he had high blood pressure. In his rather lengthy, incoherent letter, he described his symptoms and attributed his condition to a fondness for salt—especially salt beef, salt fish and salt pork. Naturally, the Reverend King was unimpressed, and he vowed that this year he wasn't going to let Jonas get away with it. Immediately upon receiving Jonas' letter, he made a trip to Dr. Templeman and got it in writing that the condition of hypertension, or high blood pressure, wouldn't hinder a person from fulfilling the duties of church sexton.

Armed with Dr. Templeman's letter, the Reverend King made a trip out to Manuel's Point to see Jonas, and shamed him into taking his turn. But the story doesn't end there.

The first morning that Jonas rang the bell, half the place scrabbled onto the road to see what it was that was afire. You see, instead of tolling the bell in a slow ding-dong rhythm, the way a bell is supposed to be rung when summoning parishioners for a service, Jonas rang it in a frantic ding-ding-ding, like one would ring it in case of an emergency. Uncle Mark White said that Jonas did it deliberately, out of spite. And then, after the Reverend King explained to Jonas the proper way of doing it, five o'clock the next morning, all of Roaring Cove was awakened by the tolling of the church bell. It was Jonas ringing it, and when asked why he had, he said he was practising for next Sunday.

As for shovelling the snow off the steps, Jonas never bothered. He simply allowed the congregation to trample in over it until it was packed down into solid ice. Thumb-On-Wrench Swyers voiced a concern at the regular vestry meeting.

"Someone is going to fall and have a limb broken," he cautioned.

"Well, if we tell him about it, we'll probably get a repeat of the bell ringing incident," commented the Reverend King.

Uncle Mark spoke up with authority, "Then, I'll be tellin' him about it." And he did.

The next Sunday morning, it was mild with freezing drizzle. There was no snow for Jonas to shovel, but the steps were a slippery glare of ice. Uncle Mark watched and waited until he was sure that Jonas wasn't going to attend to it, and up he went to the church. He found Jonas sitting in the outside porch.

"Bad old mornin', Jonas," Uncle Mark said. "The steps are awful slippery; I almost fell down getting up over them."

"Yes, they're wonderful slippery," Jonas responded.

"Should try to get a bit of salt on them, I s'pose, before the crowd shows up," Uncle Mark hinted.

Jonas pointed to the closet. "There's a bag of salt in there, Mark," he said. "You can sprinkle out some if you like."

"Indeed I won't!" Uncle Mark snapped. "You're the church sexton this month, so you do it!"

"Oh, I'm not allowed," Jonas responded calmly.

"And why is that?" Uncle Mark asked.

"Because I got high blood pressure," Jonas answered.

"What has that got to do with putting a bit of salt on the steps?" Uncle Mark asked. His annoyance was now obvious in the tone of his voice.

"It has plenty to do with it," Jonas explained. "Dr. Templeman informed me that me blood pressure was high and I'm not supposed to touch salt."

Crime in Roaring Cove

In the 1960s, a gravel road was built through Bakeapple Marsh Valley, and Roaring Cove was connected to the outside world by a cloud of dust. Uncle Mark White says that the road changed Roaring Cove forever. In the name of progress, the Sunday afternoon meal of jelly and custard, served on a lace table cloth that reeked of mothballs, was replaced by long automobile rides; pork and cabbage suppers lost out to darts and bingo, and baloney chunks and gravy gave 'way to frozen dinners.

The gravel road was one thing, but the pavement was quite another. A moratorium on the codfishery left Roaring Cove without an industry, so the government turned to tourism, and a layer of asphalt was smeared over the potholes and mud in an attempt to attract visitors. And, attract them it did; by the hundreds they invaded our little town. At first, we all thought it was a wonderful thing, but when the fish stayed away and the tourists kept coming, we grew apprehensive. We witnessed our town and lifestyle change as fish stores were transformed into craft shops and hardy fishermen became tour guides.

No one can deny that the tourist dollars were welcomed, but it was the week-long folk festival that put the kibosh on it for most people. For the third consecutive summer, Roaring

Cove became a mini Woodstock for one whole week. Campers of all shapes and sizes were set up everywhere, vendors and beer tents were erected, loud music was played into the early morning, and there was dancing in the street. And this summer, there was an unfortunate incident that caused much concern.

On the second day of the festival, Jonas Pickett left Manuel's Point to come in the harbour to check out what was going on. When he stepped on his wharf, he noticed that his punt was gone—obviously stolen. Jonas had no phone, so he hurried in along the shore to Uncle Mark's house and called the Mounties in Middleville and reported the missing punt. Now, Uncle Mark was never very fond of Jonas, but he had to sympathize with him. "We're all victims of the times," he told Jonas. "It all started when they built that bloody road. You can't open up to the whole world and not expect some bad from it."

Jonas commented that everyone thought he was foolish when he stayed on Manuel's Point by himself after everyone else moved in the harbour, but now he was glad he had.

Uncle Mark's sympathy for Jonas extended enough to steam him back out to Manuel's Point. When they came within sight of Jonas' wharf, there was the missing punt, bobbing on her collar.

"Are you sure you weren't running a drop of stuff this morning?" Uncle Mark teased.

"I tell you that punt wasn't there when I came in the harbour," Jonas retorted.

As Uncle Mark steamed alongside Jonas' punt, they noticed an unopened beer case on the cuddy with an envelope stuck to it. Inside the envelope was a ticket to the fish and brewis supper* that was being held at the festival that night, and a note that said, "Please accept these gifts for the lend of your boat."

"Well, the like a dat," Jonas said. "Sure, they're not all that bad, after all."

"Very strange indeed," Uncle Mark muttered.

As Jonas was checking his gas tank to see how much gas was burned, he said, "Call the Mounties when you gets in, Mark, and tell them I found me punt."

Now, Jonas never patronized anything that went on in Roaring Cove—that is, anything he had to pay for. But that evening, he showed up with his free ticket, and he shovelled the grub into him like it was his last meal. He openly bragged about his good fortune of free beer and ticket; but when he arrived home later that night, he got quite a surprise. The front door to his house was swinging wide open and his mattress was bottom up on the floor. His entire life's savings, over ten thousand dollars in cash, was gone. Apparently, someone knew all too well that Jonas was going to be out for the evening.

He made another quick trip into Uncle Mark's and again called the Mounties. "They're sending someone down first thing in the morning," he told Uncle Mark after he hung up.

News of Jonas' loss went through the community like a 'flu virus, and there was much alarm. This was the most

---

* A social event at which the popular fish and brewis meal is served. Fish and brewis is fish, either fresh or salted, served with brewis (soaked and boiled hard bread.

serious crime Roaring Cove had ever encountered and people began locking their doors and barring up their property. Most felt that no one from Roaring Cove could have committed such a crime, and the Mounties would have to act quickly to catch the culprits before they made their escape. But, all the next day no Mountie showed up.

Jonas could see the chances of getting his money back disappear with each passing hour. So, the first thing the next morning, he called Middleville and again reported the thief. This time, he was told that an officer had already been assigned to the case.

Jonas went home and waited all this day, but still no Mountie.

On Friday morning, he made another trip to Uncle Mark's and, for the third time, called the RCMP detachment in Middleville.

"I'd like to report a missing person!" Jonas shouted into the receiver.

Well, a missing person—that required the sergeant's attention.

"And who exactly is this person who has gone missing?" the sergeant asked when he came to the telephone.

"I don't know his name exactly," retorted Jonas. "All I know is that he is an RCMP officer, and he left Middleville three days ago to investigate a robbery in Roaring Cove, but he hasn't showed up yet."

When Jonas hung up, Uncle Mark said, "You can kiss that money good-bye, Jonas—it's long gone up over that bloody road."

Uncle Mark White Goes Moose Hunting

I went over to Thumb-On-Wrench Swyer's garage this morning to catch up on a bit of news.

"I s'pose you heard about Uncle Mark, did you?" Thumb-On-Wrench asked.

"No," says I. "What's going on with Uncle Mark?"

"Well, I don't rightly know," Thumb-On-Wrench continued. "But the wildlife officers were down there this morning and took his gun. I heard rumoured around that he got caught poaching a moose."

"That doesn't sound like Uncle Mark," I commented. I knew Uncle Mark well enough to know that he wasn't the type to take a chance on doing anything illegal. So, after lunch, I strolled down to his place to get the story firsthand.

I found him and Aunt Mae up in the potato garden behind their house. Uncle Mark was sputtering aloud that the bloody spuds were full of canker.*

"If 'tis a meal of spuds you're after, I hope you don't mind canker," Aunt Mae said when she saw me approaching.

"Well, to tell the truth, I was sort of hoping I'd get a meal

---

* A disease found in potatoes.

of moose from Uncle Mark," I said teasingly, winking at Aunt Mae.

Uncle Mark turned to face me and pushed his cap back on his head. "Hold ya tongue," he said. "You heard about the moose, didn't ya?" He drove the garden prong into the earth with authority and leaned on it. I knew I was about to get the full story.

"All last spring when we were up here settin' in this bit of garden," he said, "two moose were hangin' around the cut-over the whole time." He pointed to a big spot of cleared-out forest where the Roaring Cove men had been cutting fire-wood for years. "I said to Mae, 'Mae, I think I'll send off and get a moose license and get one of dem next fall.' And that's what I done. And, a few weeks back, I went down to the post office and, sure enough, I had the license come."

Uncle Mark pulled the prong from the ground and drove it in again, completely burying the forks. He continued, "When Mae sized up the license, she noticed that it was for a *boal* only."

Aunt Mae interrupted, "It's *bull*,* Mark, not *boal*."

"Dat's what I said—*boal*—and dat's why I'm in trouble today, because of dat bloody *boal* only license," Uncle Mark snapped. "Anyway, on Thursday morning, me and Mae went up there by the back fence. I looked up in the clearing and there was Mr. Moose, standing up as large as life. 'There he is, Mae. Do you see en?' 'I sees en,' said Mae. Now, it wasn't quite daylight, so I couldn't make out if 'twas a *boal* or not, so I waited.

---

* Referring to the bull (male) moose. Many moose licenses in Newfoundland are for the bull only.

"By and by the sky lightened and I saw the *harns*. 'Is dat *harns*, Mae?' I asked?"

Aunt Mae interrupted again, "It's *horns*, Mark, not *harns*."

"'Dat's what I said, *harns*.' Well, anyway, I wanted to be dead sure. 'You're sure 'tis *harns*, Mae?' I asked. 'Yes,' said Mae, 'tis *harns*, and if you soon don't shoot, the moose will be halfway to Kellop Harbour.' So, I raised the gun and laid her across the fence longer,* took good aim, and pulled the trigger. *Bang!* Down he come a cold junk—but 'twas one problem—da *harns* stayed up. A young birch tree.

"Now, then, you knows me and Mae wasn't in the twitter. We didn't know what to do. Here we were with a *boal* only license and a great big cow down. I wanted to clean en up and say nothing at all about it, but Mae insisted that the proper thing to do was to report it to the authorities—and dat's what I done. I called up to Middleville and told dem all about the mistake I made. In no time, the wildlife officers were down, took the moose and gun, and gave me a summons to appear in court. Now, if I had me time back, I would've followed me own mind and said nuttin' at all about it."

---

* The rail of a fence.

The Blowing Hole

I had been in Roaring Cove but a year when I made my first trip down along the shore. Rumour was circulating that Tacker Manuel had dug up some human bones while breaking up a new spot of potato ground out on Manuel's Point. I had heard it mentioned several times, but it was treated as nothing more than a normal occurrence, so I questioned Uncle Mark White about it.

"It's probably just some old Indian bones," he said.

"Indian bones?" I asked.

"Yes," replied Uncle Mark. "They're always digging up some Indian stuff out on Manuel's Point and down along the shore."

"What kind of Indians?" I asked, wild with curiosity.

"Beothucks, I s'pose," answered Uncle Mark. "The old fellers said that they used to come out on Roaring Cove Beach in the spring and summer to hunt seals and sea birds and to fish for salmon."

The Beothucks, now extinct, were Newfoundland's aboriginal people, and the thought of them having once lived near Roaring Cove made me eager to investigate.

"Will you take me there, out to Manuel's Point and down along the shore, Uncle Mark?" I asked.

"I'll be ready first thing in the morning," he responded.

It was a brilliant morning. The sun rose orange over the

Roaring Cove hills and the harbour was a pool of quicksilver. When Uncle Mark pulled the boat up on Manuel's Point beach, I had a strange feeling about this place. I felt peacefully alone, in spite of the fact that Uncle Mark was with me. I recalled a similar feeling once when I visited my grandmother's graveside.

Uncle Mark led us around a few potato gardens, and across a few empty fields to the hills above the harbour. He knew exactly where to find the narrow, granite footpath that led around the shoreline. Was this the path the Beothucks followed in their journey to the coast? Worn bare by the continuous trek of bird hunters, it wound its way around the cliffs until it eventually turned inland, across the barrens, where it faded into a thick growth of caribou moss.

On this part of the shore, solid rock cliffs rise straight out of the water like giant tombstones. Huge chunks of these cliffs are gorged away, leaving deep impressions, or gulches, as they are known in Roaring Cove. From anywhere on the footpath, one can look straight down into the gulches and into the tumultuous foam caused by the abrupt meeting of wave and rock. On days when the sea is swelling, the waves crash into the gulches and send a salt spray high into the air over the footpath.

We carefully inched our way along the cliffs and gulches. As we did, Uncle Mark identified each gulch and explained how each had acquired its name. There was Black Gulch, Treasure Chest Gulch, Red Indian Gulch and Shipwreck Gulch. Between Red Indian Gulch and Shipwreck Gulch, Uncle Mark pointed to a slab of sloping, flat rock that ran all the way into the sea.

"This is where the blowin' hole is," he said.

We climbed onto the granite slab, the only place on the

shore where it is possible to get close to the water, and slowly descended towards the sea. The flat rock was offering little resistance to the waves. They simply rolled up the rock until their momentum was spent and they lazily retreated and met their successor. On a calm day like this, one could tease a wave and race it up the slope. But on days when the sea is less playful, waves dash impetuously up the slope with deceiving speed. Many bird hunters have felt icy water rush into their rubber boots when trying to race the sea on such days, and several, over the years, have been sucked back by the undertow and lost the race forever.

Near the end of the sloping slab, a cluster of splintered, finger-shaped rocks project from the slab. On a low tide, bird hunters hide in this geological maze that they call the "birdgage." On a high tide, though, the birdgage is completely surrounded by water, and hunters waiting for a merganser to swim within range must also keep a watchful eye on the tides. On days when the sea is rough, the waves wash completely over it.

Uncle Mark and I climbed into the birdgage. Immediately, he sat on one of the several little ledges that projected like barstools from the rocks. He claimed that nature was kind when she provided the hunters with seats. I believe, though, that they were chiselled by human hands, because each is strategically located to offer a perfect view of the blowing hole.

The blowing hole is the most fascinating natural phenomenon. It is a cave that has been eroded at the low water mark into the rocks of Red Indian Gulch. On a high tide, the cave is completely submerged, but on a low tide, it bobs above the water like a half-open mouth, gasping for air. As the waves roll into the gulch, they fill the cave, forcing it to swallow the salty brine until it coughs it back. The cough is an explosive one that sends a spray of sea water high into the sunshine. It becomes magically transformed into a rainbow that fills the gulch with colour.

As Uncle Mark pointed to the blowing hole, it blew its splendour into Red Indian Gulch. I settled on one of the stone ledges and watched in silent astonishment and admiration. I became filled with reverence, feeling as if I had found what I had been looking for. Red Indian Gulch had attained its name from the Beothucks. Uncle Mark didn't know exactly why, but I knew there was a reason. They had been here; I somehow knew it. I felt something the minute I set foot on Manuel's Point; now I was certain.

For many years after, I made regular trips to the birdgage (the place I secretly called "my temple"), to observe the magnificence of the blowing hole and to sense the spirit of our first people—people of the earth.

There were times when I would sit the duration of a low tide, stare into Red Indian Gulch, and listen to the stereophonic roar of the sea as the gulches, like large brass speakers, reverberated the sound around me. Each visit was rejuvenating and therapeutic.

And then, things changed. My life became busy; my children were born, a house was built, and I stopped going. It was to be many years before I saw the birdgage again, on that fateful October day last year.

Randell Hooky from up in Kellop Harbour sold off his fishing gear and moved to the mainland. I bought his boat and motor. Uncle Mark confirmed that it was a fine seaworthy boat and, with a few alterations, could be made into a fine pleasure craft. I was anxious to get the boat to Roaring Cove and into Uncle Mark's shed before the weather turned nasty.

The boat was still tied up to Rendell's Wharf, so the easiest thing to have done was to steam it to Roaring Cove, a distance of approximately twelve miles.

It was a clear civil day when I set out. Ordinarily, I wouldn't have made the trip alone, but Winse Hillard, and any of the other fellows I would've asked to come along, were away moose hunting. I seriously thought about asking Uncle Mark; I knew he would have enjoyed it, but he is getting well up in years, so I decided against it. Besides, it was only a couple hours' steam. It was a simple matter of clearing Northern Head and following the coastline to Roaring Cove.

The wind was soft out of the southwest, and my little boat sliced through the water like the dorsal fin of a shark. I rounded Northern Head more quickly than I had anticipated and, for the first time, I got a view of the coastline from a perspective other than the one I was used to. In the distance, I could barely make out the grey of Roaring Cove Beach, like a small patch on an otherwise black cliff. The beach appeared much closer to the narrows than I thought. And, what were the shoals that were breaking far off to the east—the Branescess? I had been off Roaring Cove in boat a hundred times, and thought I had a good idea of the lie of the land, but if I had not known where I was, I would have recognized nothing. The shoreline recessed too far inward, and the Branescess were not at all where I would have pictured them to be. The thought crossed my mind that if they were not breaking, I might very well have steamed over them. But they were breaking. "Why are the Branescess breaking on a calm day?" I wondered.

As I sized up the unfamiliar scene before me, it became evident that if I skirted the shoreline as planned, it would have taken me at least an extra hour to reach Roaring Cove. I decided to steam as the crow flies, outside the Branescess and straight for Roaring Cove Beach.

When I pulled away from the shelter of Northern Head, I noticed that the sea was much rougher, but my little boat rode it like a buoyant seabird, so I visually charted my course as planned.

I had judged the Branescess at approximately one hour steam, but it was nearly two hours before I got up to them. As I swung outside to give them wide berth, I noticed heavy, black clouds on the horizon. There was a storm brewing—that explained why the Branescess were breaking. I mentally cursed the weather forecast that predicted a sunny day with light winds, but I was not alarmed. I was convinced that I could reach Roaring Cove before the storm hit.

But this was no ordinary storm. From Florida to Greenland, it was known as the storm of the century. It hit Roaring Cove with a vengeance, ripping the roofs off several stages, uprooting trees, and scattering fences throughout.

I felt the cold nip at my cheek as the wind tripped to the north. In a matter of minutes, squalls of wind, the kind that always precedes a big blow, whirled wildly, making irregular, circular patterns on the water. In the distance, whitecaps danced in fury as the wind raced towards me. I noticed that a large snow dwoi[*] was being sucked along with the wind. The storm hit like a slap of thunder. My little boat vibrated with the impact, and my cap flew from my head, skipped over the waves, and was quickly out of sight. The waves were fierce; they jumped into the boat and wet my clothes. They sprayed into my face; the salt burned my eyes.

---

* A short snow shower.

And then, the snow hit. I knew it was only a dwoi and would not last long, but it stuck to my drenched little boat and made it slippery and dangerous for me to move. It matted in my hair and eyebrows and made me more uncomfortable than I already was and, worst of all, it gave me zero visibility. I felt the need to stop and wait for the snow to pass, but I had to keep control of my boat; I had to keep her bow into the wind, and I allowed only enough throttle to do so. I did not know if I was going ahead, backwards or standing still. I sensed the danger of the situation and began to talk to myself, as I always do when I become frightened.

"I wish Uncle Mark were here," I said. "He'd know what to do. This snow can't last much longer. Everyone will be sick with worry. I don't like this one little bit. I wonder where the Branescess are?" The words were barely off my lips when the boat hit. The planks quivered as she thumped down on something solid, and there was a sharp snapping noise and the outboard rived wildly.

"I'm on the Branescess! God help me!" I shouted. "I'm finished!"

I waited to hit again. Images of jagged pieces of rock ripping through my boat raced into my mind. But it did not happen. After the boat rose and fell several more times, I knew I had hit the edge of the devious shoal and had been washed clear of them. I was not out of trouble, though. My motor was racing and was making a sickening, grinding noise. The shaft had been snapped off when it hit. I was helplessly at the mercy of the sea.

My little boat was now being tossed and hurled about like a feather on the wind. I too was being flung about uncontrollably, and I could not stay sitting. I was forced to curl up in the bottom of the boat, in water and sloppy snow.

I waited for the inevitable—for a wave to catch the boat the wrong way and flip it over or to drift ashore to be smashed against the cliffs.

Again, I talked aloud. I recited the names of my children. "I'm going to die," I told myself. "I wonder if they'll find my body. You're not afraid to die." But I *was* afraid. I was so afraid, I became nauseated and threw up.

As I had predicted, the snow did not last. It stayed only long enough to lure me onto the Branescess, then it was gone. The sun shone and warmed my body, but the wind did not slacken. This was a hurricane. I pulled myself above the gunwale of the boat and looked towards the shore. I saw the waves being smashed against the rocks, and they exploded into a white, foamy fury. This was what I was drifting into. I again settled in the bottom of the boat and listened as the sound of the shore got closer and closer. I was drifting quickly, and soon the roar of the angry sea was petrifying. I looked again and confirmed what I knew; I was very close to shore. The scene before me reminded me of when I once sailed underneath Niagara Falls in a glass-covered boat. That was when I was on vacation with my family. It was a happy time. I prayed that I was dreaming, and that I would wake up and find myself on a tour boat.

As I stared into the wall of white water, I noticed a streak of colour radiate through the flying surf. I waited for the next wave to break; again, the colour appeared. Was this the blowing hole? My survival instinct surfaced. If it were, it meant that the tide was low and that I was close to the granite slab—the only place on the shore where there was even a remote chance of landing a boat without having it smashed to pieces. "Maybe, just maybe," I thought, "I can ride a wave up the granite slope and get close enough to jump to the land."

For the first time since hitting the Branescess, a wave of hope flooded through me. It was a long shot, but there was no other plan, so I stopped thinking about dying and filled my mind with the details of my plan. I grabbed the sculling oar and pushed it into the rowlock mounted on the stern; I sat upright in the bottom of the boat and worked frantically to control my direction. If this were the blowing hole, I had to keep it to my right side. I had to clear the birdgage, but I also knew that if I kept too far to the left, I would have entered Shipwreck Gulch. If that happened, I knew there was no escape. I kicked off my boots, grabbed a rope, and tied it around my waist, coiling the remainder over my shoulder.

Suddenly, I was in the spray, and it settled around me. There, ahead of me, looming up like a runway, was the granite slab. The waves were hitting it, churning white and running its entire length. I knew I had to catch a wave just right. I struggled to point my boat towards the shore. Finally, I was in position; I counted the waves. One... two... three... four. Number five picked up my little boat as if it were a cork and escorted it up the granite slab. I tugged and pulled on the sculling oar to stay straight. I could see the land getting closer and closer. I praised my efforts and readied myself to jump.

I was almost there when I heard the scraping, scratching noise of the motor on the rock bottom. I cursed aloud my stupidity; I had not thought to tip the damn motor forward. It dragged over the rock and grounded the boat, not ten feet from the land and safety. I scrambled to jump anyway into the water, but before I could, the boat was jerked back by the undertow. It was quickly pulled into the turmoil water where the undertow met the approaching waves, and it was spun in circles. It was broadside when the next wave hit. I felt the boat lift and tip, and I was hurled into the turbulence.

The chill of the frigid water numbed me, and I felt that death would be instantaneous. The pressure of the wave pinned me to the rock bottom, and my chest and back felt as if the two were meeting. As my lungs were about to explode, the pressure slackened, and the life vest (the one Uncle Mark had insisted that I wear) brought me to the surface like a buoy at the end of a fisherman's lobster pot. I gulped in air, squeezed my eyes shut, and again held my breath as I was thrust around in somersaults.

Suddenly, I hit something solid, and a piercing pain shot through my side. I felt the water run away from me, and I gasped in more air. Each breath sent a sharp pain straight to my heart. Slowly, afraid of what I would see, I opened my eyes. I immediately knew where I was; the sea had washed me into the birdgage. I was in my temple.

"I must get higher. The next wave will wash over me," I said aloud, but in a whisper because of the pain. I held my rib cage in both hands and crawled to the highest splinter of rock. The next wave washed around my knees and the mist settled around me. I was safe, but not for long. The tide was rising, and when it did, I knew it would break over the birdgage.

There was no escape. I could not have made it to shore, even if the sea became calm. My ribs were obviously broken, and with any movement I could have punctured a lung—if I had not done so already. I simply had to wait for the tide to rise...wait to die.

With exasperating pain, I loosened the rope that was still coiled around my shoulder, and I lashed myself to the rock. I would not gratify the sea the opportunity of claiming my body. I would be found lashed high in my temple.

I lay still and waited, staring into Red Indian Gulch. The blowing hole was more magnificent than I had ever seen it. It exploded into the gulch with passion and, even in the face of death, I found myself hypnotized by its splendour. Through the kaleidoscope of colour, I saw the face of the cliff. It moved as the coloured spray drifted over it and, like a giant cinema screen, it played out life's drama.

I saw the faces of my children, and I saw my wife. I saw myself stepping off the steamer onto the wharf in Roaring Cove that very first time. I saw Uncle Mark standing the full length of the cliff. He was wearing his legion blazer and tam, and he was wearing a poppy.

I saw barely-clad red men, with spears in their hands, emerge from the cliff. Red women, with babies feeding at their breasts, followed them. They hovered in the mist and, with waving gestures, beckoned me to follow them. They disappeared the way they had come.

I saw the cliff as it opened like a womb and gave birth to a child. I was the child. I was red. I was naked and crying. A set of aged and wrinkled hands wrapped around me and lifted me; they were the hands of my grandmother. Suddenly, I was no longer a child; I was a small boy. I was playing on my grandmother's back bridge, and I was swinging on a screen door.

Then I saw my grandmother. She was young, and she was on a flake, gathering huge yaffles of dried codfish in her apron. For a moment, the spray settled and the sun washed the cliff a deathly white. The face of the cliff became my grandmother's face, the face I had seen lying in a coffin. Impressions and projections of the rock sculptured it perfectly, as cracks and lines in the cliff formed wrinkles and aged her. She opened her eyes slowly, a peaceful smile formed on her lips, and the image melted into the cliff.

My soul sank into the crevices and a surge of strength and spirituality rushed through me. I was no longer afraid to die. I felt the spirit of the land, and I became one with the rock to which I was tied. I realized that the force pushing the water from the blowing hole was the same force that was pushing the blood through my veins. This was a message of eternal salvation; I closed my eyes and drifted away—out of danger.

I awoke to the sensation of water rushing around me and to the sound of voices calling my name. I looked to the top of Red Indian Gulch, and through the mist I saw a small group of men. I recognized Uncle Mark's form among them. They were Roaring Cove men; they had come for me!

Expertly and quickly, lines were thrown into the birdgage and fastened securely to shore. Like acrobats, men slid down the ropes. Blocks and tackles were set in place, and I was wrapped in an old fishing net and hoisted to shore.

I remembered nothing else about the rescue. When I became aware and conscious, I was in a hospital bed in Middleville, and my wife was standing over me, smiling down at me. I reached up and held her hand.

"I almost lost you," she said.

"How did they find me?" I asked. As I spoke, the familiar pain jabbed at my side.

"It was Uncle Mark," she replied. "He knew—somehow."

"The man's a saint," I said with a smile.

It was mid-morning the next day when Uncle Mark and Aunt Mae showed up at my hospital room. I caught the smell of homemade soup coming from the little parcel that Aunt

Mae was carrying. "Here ya are, me son," she said, laying the parcel on the night stand next to my bed. "Nothing like a drop of fresh beef soup to nourish an ailing body."

Uncle Mark sat on the foot of my bed and squeezed my foot through the bedclothes. "I'm gonna have to teach ya how to watch the weather signs," he said.

"How did you know, Uncle Mark?" I asked. "How did you know I was in the birdgage?"

"I didn't fer sure," he responded. "Common sense told me it was one of two things—either you were in the water and drowned, or you made it to land. The only place to land a punt on that shore is on the granite slab, and I knew you knew that."

"You're a smart man, Uncle Mark," I said. "And lucky for me you are."

He flushed red with the embarrassment of the compliment. "I'm only a simple man," he said.

"A simple man," I repeated. "A simple man of the earth."

*"Burn your boats!" was the big cry of the 1960s.
Aunt Daisy Snelgrove, deaf on the left side since birth,
heard
"Burn Your Goats!"*

1996, (20" X 16") oil on canvas

BURN YOUR BOATS

Aunt Daisy's Spuds

Alfie Lambert be a devilskin, and Uncle Mark
    is quite the ticket
But never was there a sleeveen as bad as Jonas Pickett.
Lie, cheat and swindle, and steal from innocent souls,
And according to Uncle Mark, too lazy to pick his own nose.

Now, all hands in Roarin' Cove is up to his sly ways,
So we ignore him and listen to nothing that he says
But whenever we get a chance to get one back on him
We surely do avail of it, and give a dose of his own medicine.

Like Aunt Daisy Snelgrove, Roarin' Cove's hypochondriac
Did when she was in the hospital with her gallbladder attack.
She got one over on old Jonas; I can state as fact
'Cause I was there to witness it, the most lovely of any act.

Now, a hard-working woman was Aunt Daise, if there
    ever was one.
Grew twelve barrels of spuds last fall and did it just for fun.
She lugged them into the cellar in spite of feeling mighty poor.
It was this that brought on her attack, of it she knew for sure.

Now, she was taken to the hospital up there in Middleville,
And news came back to us that Aunt Daise was really very ill.

She had taken a turn for the worse and was failing fast.
Uncle Mark said, "Not to worry. Aunt Daise died several
    times in the past."

They said she was confused and her mind was nearly gone,
So we went to see her, thinking surely they were wrong.
Now, I know you'll never guess, so I'll tell you straight away.
Who it was that went to visit Aunt Daisy every single day.

'Twas none other than old Jonas himself, so the nurses told us.
And each day he made a special trip on Sam Whiffen's bus.
Uncle Mark was suspicious, and he had good right to be
'Cause old Jonas did nothing for anyone, unless it was
    for a fee.

"He's after something," said Uncle Mark. "I have no doubt
    in my mind.
Preying on a sick woman most likely—that's Jonas Pickett's
    kind."
"Schoolmaster," he said to me, "I tell you there's
    something very wrong.
I think you should visit Aunt Daise and find out what is
    going on."

So I took Uncle Mark's advice and visited Aunt Daise the
    very next day.
We talked a little bit and I brought up Jonas in a casual sort
    of way.
Says I, "Nice of Jonas to come to visit, all the way
    from another place.
But Uncle Mark says for you beware of him 'cause he's
    quite the case."

"I'm a sick woman," said Aunt Daise. "But I'm not all that
    stun,
And you don't have to warn me of the likes of Jonas Pickett,
    my son.
The minute I saw him coming through the door I could see
His black eyes scheming and I knew he was after
    something from me.

"And 'tis me spuds he's after, me son, of that I have no doubt.
'Cause he up and told me that me spuds would spoil
    before I get out.
Said it would be a sin to let them sprout and decay
And that it would be better if I gave them all away.

"He said he'd like to have them and perhaps we could
    strike a deal
'Cause his spuds were all canker this year and he wouldn't
    save a meal.
Now he thinks me mind is gone, but he had better think twice
'Cause I know all too well, Old Jonas never set a spud in his
    life."

Now, as we were talking, upon the door there came a rap
And in slinked old Jonas, just like the cellar rat.
He threw me a black look when he saw that I was there
And he sat by Aunt Daisy's bed in the big old hospital chair.

He dipped into a nut bowl that was sitting on the stand.
"Is there anything I can get ya? I'm here to help in any way
    I can."
He buttered up Aunt Daise and was as nice as pie,
Enough to give the dog's arse the heartburn, and that's no lie.

He made small talk to me, as if he had nothing to gain
And he dipped into the nut bowl over and over again.
He never once mentioned spuds, turnips, or even peas,
But he kept dropping hints to say it was time for me to leave.

Well, I settled in my seat and was as comfortable as could be.
"I'll outstay you," thought I, 'cause I knew the bus left
    sharply at three.
Finally, when he saw that I was firmly planted in my seat,
Dipping into the bowl, he said, "I'd better go. I'll soon
    have your **spuds** all eat.

"**Nuts**...I mean **nuts**...I'll soon have your nuts all gone!"
And he flushed all red when he realized he said it wrong.
"Oh, that's all right," said Aunt Daisy with a grin and a sigh,
"You can eat the whole lot, if you like, Jonas, and
    I'll tell you why.

"I've lost weight since my attack, and I haven't gained
    back a bit.
My cheeks are hollow, my jaws have shrunk, and my
    false teeth don't fit.
I can't chew up the nuts, you see, and I'd like for you to know
That I can only suck the chocolate off and
    spit them back in the bowl."